P9-CFQ-941

What It Takes

Speak Up, Step Up, Move Up

What It Takes

Speak Up, Step Up, Move Up

A Modern Woman's Guide
to Success in Business

Amy Henry

St. Martin's Press

New York

ISBN 0-312-34019-2
EAN 978-0312-34019-3

10   9   8   7   6   5   4   3   2

To my parents,
Bob and Sue Rash,
I love you very much

Contents

Foreword

Amy Henry's life has changed dramatically since her experience with me on *The Apprentice*. She had a successful career in the high-tech sector before interviewing for the opportunity of a lifetime—a chance to work directly for me in a prestigious role at the Trump Organization.

On the show, I continuously watched in amazement at her astonishing victory record—ten wins in a row. No matter where she went, her team always won. Was it Amy's leadership ability, her team spirit, her positive attitude, her work ethic? I think it was a combination of many traits that demonstrated her solid business savvy. She made it further than any other female contestant and was one of the final four to face me in the boardroom. During *The Apprentice*, I consistently called Amy the team MVP because she was always the first-round draft pick and the first person stolen every time I reshuffled the teams until I told everyone, "Enough!" By telling me Amy was the first person they wanted on their team, her competitors only made her look better. I thought it was a terrible move; I'd never do that if I were in their shoes.

I must admit I was not at all surprised to see Amy rise above the competition on the show given her past successes off the show.

Amy's real-world experience working with customers, colleagues, and executives from start-up companies and Fortune 500 corporations gave her the skills and preparation to excel.

When Amy told me she was writing a book, I was delighted that she had already learned my number one rule of business: tell people about your successes or else they will never know about them. Amy goes many steps further and shares lessons she has learned from mistakes as well as victories. Business is tough, and her advice can help you stay focused, speak directly, take risks, be a leader, earn respect, and think big, as well as get the recognition you deserve and the money you are worth. She may even share a few words of wisdom she learned from The Donald.

I predict Amy will be a success at whatever she does. She's got intelligence, discipline, pragmatism, and beauty, both inside and out. This woman has her bases covered, and I have to say that she was right to name her book after something I once said about her: "Amy's got *what it takes*."

—Donald J. Trump

Acknowledgments

There have been so many people who provided guidance, advice, education, training, and support as I grew—and continue to grow—into the businesswoman I want to be. My colleagues and clients at Sabre, Commerce One, and BetweenMarkets have taught me much, and I thank each of you. While I am not able to cite every person from my past that has shaped me professionally, there are a few I would like to single out.

I'm especially thankful to all my family and friends for their continuous love, patience, and support. Thanks to my mother, Sue Rash, for teaching me to remain optimistic, positive, and focused on achieving whatever I set my mind to. You have taught me the true meaning of a "can-do" attitude. To my father, Bob Rash: thanks for teaching me the ABC's of business. You created my business mind and shaped many of my professional standards; your guidance has helped me concentrate in my career and thoroughly evaluate each move I make—always balancing risk and reason. To Josh Rash, for being my brother and inspiring me with your focus. To my sister, Jessica Rash, who encourages me to always be true to myself and is a constant example of spirit and positive energy. To my grandmother, Jo Rash, who motivates me to stay balanced and active, and to my other grandmother, Dessi Lee Gibbs, who taught me how to be an independent woman.

I'd like to thank Rob LaPlante, casting director for *The Apprentice*, for picking me out of hundreds of thousands of applicants and vociferously promoting me to his production staff. Thanks to Mark Burnett for being the genius behind *The Apprentice*, and to the entire MJB Production staff for their hard work and dedication to excellence. To Donald Trump for bringing *The Apprentice* to life and teaching me invaluable lessons for success in business.

I'd like to thank my agent, Maura Teitlebaum, for her faith and perseverance and for taking a giant leap with me to fight for this book and make it happen. To my publisher, Sally Richardson at St. Martin's Press: thanks for listening to my vision and saying, "Let's make it happen *now!*" To my editor, Nichole Argyres, who provided exceptional feedback, guidance, and coaching. To Laura Henson at Escada for always ensuring I look my very best. And thanks to Michael Deane for your tolerance and constant reinforcement throughout this whirlwind experience.

I also extend my heartfelt appreciation to all the women who shared their insights and experiences with me for the book, and to my male colleagues and managers who, over the years, framed many of the bold ideas in this book's pages. Many of these friends and colleagues are named in the book. Some names have been changed or withheld.

And last but not least, I'd like to thank my collaborator, Joanne Gordon, who has helped bring my voice to life by patiently and diligently shaping everything I write and challenging me to think and speak bigger and bolder. Thank you so much for your wisdom.

What It Takes

Speak Up, Step Up, Move Up

Introduction

For years people have told me I'm "more man than woman" when it comes to business. I was never sure whether to take that statement as a compliment or an insult, but I've come to understand what colleagues mean when they describe me that way. They don't mean I lack femininity—please, I love my bleached blond hair, fitted clothes, high heels, and slight Southern accent. They mean I'm confident, assertive, persistent, tough, headstrong, and ambitious—all qualities traditionally associated with business*men*, not business-*women*.

But both men and women need those qualities to excel, and if women want to move up in their jobs, we must be aggressive, confident, vocal, and proud of our accomplishments. Women do not, I repeat *not*, have to act like men to succeed in the business world—stereotypically female traits such as listening, relationship building, and empathy are critical to meeting business goals. But to compete and thrive, we must combine male and female behaviors: assertiveness as well as hard work, confidence as well as charm, and decisiveness as well as intuition.

My own ability to take risks and express myself—as well as work compatibly with teammates and avoid pettiness—helped make me one of the final four contestants on *The Apprentice* in addition to bringing me success in my career. Now, I want to empower you to get what you want from your career. Whether you are new to the workplace and haven't yet found a mentor to whisper business secrets in your ear, or if you have been working for some time and are having trouble climbing the corporate ladder as quickly as you think you should be, I am confident *What It Takes* will provide a few new ideas and strategies to help you.

Competence Is Not Enough

I was not uncomfortable being the "last woman standing" on *The Apprentice*—I'm used to being the sole woman standing among men. I grew up in a neighborhood where I was the only girl. I was surrounded by men in graduate school. I spent eight years in the male-dominated technology industry, and at my last job I was the only full-time female employee in a company of more than 30 men. *The Apprentice* was actually the first time in years I had worked with so many women.

In every postshow interview people asked me if I had a strategy, and my response every time was no. I was just combining my knowledge with the business skills I had observed, adopted, and sharpened after years working with men. Again, I'm not saying you must behave like a man to get what you want at work. What I am saying is that, long ago, men wrote the rules and set the standards that dominate in today's business environments. In order to succeed in what is still a male-run business world, women need to know what those rules and standards are—and then shape them to fit our own spirit, style, and personality.

While I am still growing in my own career and continuing to learn, I do know this: competence is not enough. Moving up in today's workplace takes much more than intellect, hard work, and education. You must also:

- build relationships with superiors
- speak up on behalf of your needs and accomplishments
- step up to challenging assignments that demonstrate your skills
- use rather than hide your charm and intuition
- value your work and ask for the money you deserve
- let objectivity rather than emotion guide your workplace behavior
- make yourself and your achievements known

I know that you, as a reader of this book, have the mind, the work ethic, and the desire to excel, and I trust that you are responsible, professional, and capable. All you need now are strategies and concrete techniques to help you flourish in today's workplace. While I cannot tell you how to do your specific job, I can empower you with tips that you can modify to fit your own style and get what you want from work, be it a promotion, more money, respect, new assignments, or access to greater opportunities.

However you desire to move up at work, know this: you can control your own work setting to prevent stereotypes, colleagues, and managers or even fear, jealousy, and frustration from controlling you. The advice and real-life examples in *What It Takes* don't come just from my own experience but from other successful working women and workplace experts. My goal is to help you take a fresh, informed look at your own working life, become more aware of your current work behaviors, and improve them so that you, too, can move up in your career.

Growing Up

My suburban, middle-class neighborhood in Arlington, Texas, was full of families, and all the kids on my block—the ones who played kickball and hide-and-seek, built forts and rode Big Wheels—were boys. That didn't stop me from playing, and I can still hear the boys whining, "Aw, does Amy have to play?" Even though I was usually the last one chosen for teams, and even though I wasn't as strong or fast, I always tried to keep up with the boys, climbing trees or stealing second base until the sun went down and I'd hear my mother call me to dinner.

In retrospect, I was not just having fun and learning how to play with the boys on my block, I was learning how to work with boys in the business world. Those childhood games helped me cultivate a competitive spirit, plus I absorbed unwritten rules about how teams work together to reach goals. I learned to stand up for myself, and I learned how to fight with people on the field and then go jump in the pool and pal around with them after the game. I learned not to cry when the boy next door yelled, "You suck" after I struck out. And, even though I was not an extraordinary athlete, I learned that winning was the goal. As I grew older, my habits did not change, and my competitive spirit only intensified.

Much of the confidence I exuded outside my home was a result of what went on inside my home. My father had been a professional football player for two years, and so I grew up with sports on television and sports in conversation. My mother (she and Dad met in third grade and married after college) was the confident cheerleader of the house, always supporting me and my younger brother and sister. Yet my parents did not push me. In school, my competitive nature seemed to fuel itself, and I worked hard to get good grades. Mom and Dad never reprimanded me for getting a few B's—I beat myself up enough in my quest for a consistent 4.0

grade point average—I was simply competing with myself, and I wanted to win.

I didn't know many women who worked full-time, other than one of my grandmothers who was a bank vice president. My mother was a stay-at-home mom, as were all the other mothers on my block. Yet my family instilled in me a strong work ethic. My father worked for the government for almost thirty years as an agent for the Bureau of Alcohol, Tobacco, and Firearms, and was proud of his job status, financial security, and work-and-life balance. My mother always told me I could achieve whatever I wanted, as long as I was willing to put in the effort. My other grandmother, who worked as a church office manager, recalls that my quest for money and success started at an early age, and she always reminds me of the time I asked her, "Granny, when I grow up, can I buy this church?"

Anxious to start working, I "founded" my first company when I was about six (a lemonade stand, yes, but it was profitable), and soon I was baby-sitting at an age when most kids still had sitters—I even marketed myself by distributing flyers advertising my $2-an-hour baby-sitting services. By the time I graduated from Texas A&M University, I had worked every summer: I sold programs at the ballpark, served patrons as a waitress, manned the front desk at an athletic club, tested beef in a meatpacking plant, sold chocolates and caramel-covered apples at a candy store, assisted a wedding photographer, managed the office of a psychology clinic, sold encyclopedias over the phone, and was an intern at the corporate offices of Mary Kay cosmetics and the retail chain Color Tile. As for all the money I earned, I saved almost every penny. After college, I took a job working in the marketing department of the Bombay Company and went on to receive my master's degree in business administration from Texas Christian University. By the time I had my MBA, I was more than ready to move on to the real world of business.

My Workplace Reality, before TV

I launched my career right before the height of the Internet boom and, full of ambition, focused my aspirations on the technology industry. I was fascinated with the technology sector because it attracted really smart people, the environment was extremely fast-paced, and most companies paid extremely well. While you do not have to know a thing about technology to get great tips from *What It Takes*, you may want to know about my work background so you understand the context in which I formed the advice and ideas in these pages.

I was not, and never will be, a techie—I cannot install complex software programs or design any type of network architecture (and when it comes to developing software applications, I am clueless). But I have served as both a project manager and an account director supervising large customer engagements and overseeing many complex, multimillion-dollar software implementations. Essentially, my roles have been to serve as the liaison between the software provider (my company) and the customer. Because business software is complicated and customized to each client's needs, my job was to manage a barrage of changes, problems, and, yes, a lot of bitching from all parties. I've often described customer management work as a juggling act—you must clearly communicate information to everyone, from computer developers to CEOs; assess client requirements and recommend appropriate solutions; analyze business processes and translate them into technical requirements; build timelines and manage work closely to ensure teams meet deadlines; evaluate risks and bring up sticky issues; hire, manage, and allocate staff; ensure long-term customer satisfaction; up-sell new solutions to accounts; and maintain relationships with each customer. All told, I've worked on close to 50 projects with companies ranging in size from start-ups to the likes of IBM, Merrill

Lynch, Morgan Stanley, Lockheed Martin, Eastman Chemical, Columbia HCA, Goldman Sachs, Accenture, Bain & Company, EDS, and BellSouth, to name a few. The assignments have taken me to Los Angeles, San Francisco, New York City, Boston, Atlanta, Nashville, Dallas, and cities throughout Europe.

My first job out of graduate school was as a business analyst and product manager with Sabre in its leisure marketing department based in Dallas–Fort Worth. Sabre is best known for its global distribution company, which enables travel agents to book air, car, hotel, cruise, and tour reservations electronically. During my first year at Sabre, I analyzed travel-booking trends for tours and managed my department's budget.

Eventually I transferred within Sabre to the East Coast and began working with the company's hot Internet start-up division, Sabre Business Travel Solutions, helping clients build web-based systems so corporate travelers could book their own arrangements over the Internet. It was 1997, the so-called Internet economy was heating up, and so was my own Internet fever. After two years at Sabre, I left to join a start-up company called Commerce One. Over the next several years, Commerce One expanded rapidly, went public, and became one of the most influential builders of on-line marketplaces, also known as trade exchanges. Our software solutions linked buyers and suppliers into on-line trading communities so companies in the same industry could buy and sell supplies through one common hub. Between 2000 and 2001, Commerce One was one of the Internet's highest fliers.

As Internet companies started to collapse in 2001, Commerce One, unfortunately, also suffered, and by 2003 I had survived more than eight rounds of layoffs. Eventually, I decided to leave the company and began working at BetweenMarkets, a young Austin-based company whose supply chain software let companies better manage their product distribution and fulfillment systems.

Working in this 30-person company, I was the sole liaison between customers and the company's technology development team. I also managed the software implementation for BetweenMarkets's first large corporate customer.

Then, on a hot summer day last June, I was driving to Dallas–Fort Worth to visit my family when a girlfriend called my mobile phone and told me she had heard auditions were being held in Dallas for a reality show called *The Apprentice*. I'd never heard of the show, and I rarely watched television, but the show's premise—*Survivor* for businesspeople—had my name all over it. The next thing I knew, I was living in a suite at Trump Tower with 15 strangers, and my life took an amazing professional turn. Thanks to Mark Burnett Productions and Donald Trump, I had a rare opportunity to showcase my business acumen and professional skills on a national platform. *What It Takes* is not about *The Apprentice*, but *The Apprentice* is all about *What It Takes*.

What It Takes

From my days managing multimillion-dollar software projects to selling $20 glasses of lemonade on *The Apprentice*, and from playing with boys on my block to working in male-dominated industries and offices, I have become convinced that the secret to moving up and getting what you want at work is not about being the smartest person or the hardest worker—it is about how well we communicate, whether we take on challenges and risks, and to what degree we take control over our own working lives. Women do not (yet) rule the business world, and we still have to fight if we want to play with those who do. It does not take a man or male traits to be successful in business—it takes a gutsy, confident, graceful woman who uses empowering strategies to move up at work.

Work It, Baby

The Power of Networking

There was a time, earlier in my career, when I assumed that if I simply worked hard, kept my head down, and stayed out of office politics, I'd get ahead. I believed, as many women do, that my effort and talent would speak for themselves. Promotions and raises would steadily come my way as my boss saw the fruits of my labor. So, I spent most days hunkered down in my cube or working diligently at client sites. Forget going to lunch with colleagues or spending a few minutes at the beginning of my day to have coffee in the break room. I was too busy writing proposals, updating project plans, and creating detailed PowerPoint presentations.

As time passed, I began to notice an annoying little phenomenon: the men around me *were* going to lunch. They were leaving early to go golf, and they were yakking in the boss's office about the latest football scores. More annoying still, they certainly didn't seem to be suffering professionally because of it. As for most of the women around me (well, the few who existed in the predominately male technology environment), they operated more like I did, and they, too, seemed to be working harder—or at least longer—than most of the men. We all seemed to harbor the same "If I don't do it, it won't get done" attitude. We were always focused on the work, and we disappeared into our little worlds to churn out the best possible results. Yes, we emerged triumphant, expectations met. But there was one big mistake we all made: we were confident that our work—in and of itself—was the single driver to boost us up the career ladder.

We were wrong. We were suckers.

I realized sooner rather than later, thankfully, that moving up is not just about the work you do but also about whom you know and who knows what you are doing. In other words, women need to develop a network of smart, influential people who are familiar with their skills and accomplishments, who provide career advice, and who alert them to professional opportunities. Building this network requires not just getting out of your office but adjusting your communication style and channels—how you express yourself and to whom—so that you connect with and impress the most influential people, those who can promote you, approve projects, listen to and act on your ideas, and accommodate your requests. Some call such deliberate behavior "politicking," and they may be right. But it's not a bad thing. Networking is also not a social, side activity but a conscious effort to connect with people who can, in a variety of ways, assist your career.

Some of you are probably rolling your eyes at the mere notion of playing the networking game. Perhaps you despise the concept and think networking and politicking are insincere, flirtatious, two-faced, brownnosing behaviors. After all, a woman's work and talent should stand on their own. Or perhaps you already know you should be networking but have struggled with just how to initiate relationships.

Whether you deem yourself above networking or are simply confused by it, think of networking as a business tool that helps you build a fourth relationship category. You already have friends and family and, perhaps, a significant other. Now you need business connections—work associates with whom business is the unabashed basis of your relationship, people with whom you discuss company news, industry trends, business tactics, and topics particular to your line of work. Some of these business connections will become social friends, but at the end of the day most of these relationships are about work, and these people won't have the same loyalty to you as family and friends. Business connections are strategic relationships, for both you and the other person.

Unless you go out of your way to initiate and cultivate these professional relationships, they will not exist. They will dwindle, and then the only person available to help you move up will be, well, you. And you can't move up alone.

Networking Is Not a Dirty Word

Diane Danielson, founder of the Downtown Women's Club, a women's networking organization, points out that too many women mistakenly consider networking a superficial way to sell themselves or as lightweight chitchat that lets them "bond" with colleagues. Wrong!

First, networking is not about going to organized happy hours to dole out your phone number and collect as many business cards as you can stuff into your purse. And it does not have to be some insincere, phony activity like sorority rush (although I must admit that, when I was in college, pretending to be interested in a rushee's conversation about where she purchased her larger-than-life floral bow *did* prepare me for conversing with strangers in the real world).

Networking is not a card grab or a brainless gab but an effective way to meet people. It is no more underhanded than going to a party, to a bar, or on-line to meet someone you want to date. Networking is serious business because it gives you access to *informa-*

tion and *people* that can improve your career in the short and long term. If you refuse to believe in networking's value or to treat it like a serious business tool, then my message to you is this: I'll see you in ten years, when you're still sitting at the same desk in the same job and I'm your boss's boss.

Still not convinced of the power of networking? Then try to think of it from a different angle. The reality is that networking is no more than building strong relationships with people, and that's something many women not only do naturally but better than most men. The trick is doing it in a professional context and in a manner that both men and women can relate and respond to.

If you want to move up, networking is simply necessary. And even the most introverted and shy among us can master it. One of my favorite, and most palatable, takes on networking is to approach it as research. It's as much about collecting data as it is about talking and sharing. Think of it as productive gossip: a way to learn about important topics related to your company and your industry (and ultimately your career) from coworkers, managers, and business contacts.

◆ **What it takes:** Drop the networking bias. Networking is no more than building relationships, researching, and conversing with colleagues. There's nothing distasteful about that.

Network Outside Your Immediate Sphere of Influence

Think of *network* not just as a verb but as a noun: your network, a concrete entity that you structure one lunch, one cocktail party, one conversation at a time. That network consists of several levels, not just people to interact with every day. Ian Hollingworth, my primary client contact at Quadrem, a company that runs an electronic marketplace for the mining industry, puts it this way: the workplace is not a pure meritocracy. In other words, merit alone won't allow you to move up. Men know this; women find it hard to accept because it seems unfair. When I worked with Ian I was connected from the highest levels of the company to the "get-the-job-done" level, as he likes to say. Ian thinks my company-wide network helped me excel, and I have to agree. Not only did it help me accomplish day-to-day tasks, it also gave me an opportunity to sell my company's services to other Quadrem departments, which I did.

Also, recognize that networking is not just about the person you are speaking with, but that person's own extended network and contacts. Once you establish a relationship with one person, you have access to his or her network, and so on and so on.

◆ **What it takes:** Don't limit yourself to networking in only one division of a company. Maintain contacts throughout an organization, and your field of opportunity widens.

Play Up

Relationships do not replace quality work, but in my opinion, quality work alone will not necessarily further your career. Networking is as important as the work itself.

In one of my performance reviews while I was working on a project in Atlanta for BellSouth, my account director, Janie, cautioned me, "Amy, while your performance is great, I have one word of advice. You need to learn to *play up*." When I asked what she meant, she said that I needed to start associating myself—and socializing—with people above me at the company. I already had a lot of work friends, ranging from administrative assistants to the consultants I managed, but most of them worked for me or were at my job level. Janie told me I was in a dangerous spot by avoiding the so-called big boys. "If you are going to spend time outside of the office with colleagues, make sure they are the right people," she said again. By "right," Janie meant superiors who have the power to promote you.

Initially, I was frustrated by her comment and thought she was telling me to kiss up to management. I had spent a lot of time not only on my own workload but also getting to know the programmers and other consultants who worked for me, making sure I was more than just a faceless account manager who barked orders. The relationship building was paying off, and I not only enjoyed my colleagues but also was working well with them to meet client deadlines ahead of schedule—something people before me had difficulty accomplishing. People knew me as a person, not just some demanding "bitch" who showed up and gave commands whenever she needed something. My relationships with my colleagues helped me exceed the client's expectations, which meant the client was available as a company reference to other potential customers, which kept my bosses at home happy, too.

I wanted credit for that, among other accomplishments, but— and this is when I came to understand what Janie meant—those accomplishments did not matter unless someone in a decision-making position knew about them and could associate my name and face with them. If I wanted to be promoted, and I did, I had to spend more time with people who had power over my next assignment, my next promotion, and my future. And why is this important? Because if the right people don't know you are doing the work, you'd better believe that someone else will take credit for it. (We'll get more into the importance of making yourself—and your work—known in chapter seven.)

Janie did not leave me to my own devices. She invited me to participate in presentations to clients as well as to the executive management team, and she included me in gatherings outside the office with the more senior crowd. When the executives from our company came to Atlanta to meet with my client, BellSouth, Janie invited me to join them for dinner to discuss client issues. Before that dinner, senior management had no idea who I was—they didn't even know my name, much less what I did for the company. It was the first time senior people heard about how I, and not my boss, was taking care of our customers. I guarantee you, this was not the last time I got out of my office and into the world. My networking *up* had officially begun.

◆ **What it takes:** Recognize the value of creating relationships with superiors who have the power to promote you.

Play Down

Playing up means extending your network to people who are above you in the chain of command. Playing down means networking with everyone else: colleagues and subordinates, even people in other departments. It's been said that the best way to get to the boss is to befriend his or her administrative assistant, because the assistant controls the boss's schedule. Sometimes, the people who have power and valuable information to share are not necessarily the ones with fancy titles or big offices. At one healthcare client I worked with, I came to realize that a mid-level manager in his late twenties, Kelly, loved to keep his hand on the pulse of all aspects of the company: who was promoted, who had quit, who was handed a new assignment. It was almost a hobby for him, and finding out what he knew became a habit for me as well. Whenever I came to town to visit my client, my first stop—before I sat down with my client, the chief operating officer—was to Kelly's cubicle. Kelly filled me in on the hot issues of the day: who was moving up, who was moving out, what problems everyone was moaning about. By chatting with Kelly first, I was always more prepared to meet with executives and better able to target my company's services to meet their needs.

◆ **What it takes:** Building relationships with influential players in the organization is valuable, regardless of title and rank.

Network Outside Your Company

You should also develop a web of contacts and professional friends outside your organization. Its mere existence will make you a stronger player inside your company because when you have an external network, you do not feel quite as shackled to your current employer. Just ask one businesswoman:

> *The stronger your network of people outside your company, the more power you have inside your company. I am in a job today that I know I can quit if I so desire, and for whatever reason. I can walk out of this building and have a job tomorrow, and I never have to post my resume on-line. Always be in a position where you are not desperate. My boss and my colleagues know I choose to be here; they do not choose me to be here. That is power.*

If lawyers only networked with other lawyers, how would they find new clients? My position in the technology sector does not mean I should reach out only to people in my profession; experts in other fields may have fresh ideas, perspectives, and opportunities to pass on. A good reason to find helpful people outside your immediate industry circle comes from Trish Murphy, a singer in Austin, Texas. While Trish has a rich network of fellow performers, her mentor—the person who gives her more career advice than anyone—is a retired female technology executive. Instead of focusing on Trish's art, the mentor helps Trish focus on keeping that art a profitable business. "I've learned that the music business is not that different from other industries," says Trish. "My mentor may be in technology, but she has actually helped me create business opportunities for myself." What's more, by having a mentor outside her industry, Trish says she can be more honest and open, and she gets a truly objective perspective—something she might not get from a fellow musician.

I recently saw the value of cross-industry networks when I spoke to a local group of young entrepreneurs. Every few months, local business owners from all types of companies get together, sit around tables, and talk about their respective businesses' problems. They swap ideas and expertise. The president of an engineering company may have a marketing idea for a local restaurant owner, and vice versa. At the very least, all the entrepreneurs get a fresh perspective about how to grow their own company.

◆ **What it takes:** Establish relationships with people outside your company and industry.

Listen Up and Don't Interrupt

Whether you play up or play down or play outside your office, you must always listen. The good news is that women tend to be better and more patient listeners than men because as girls we're taught that it's rude to interrupt other people when they talk. While speaking your mind in many work situations is crucial to moving up, it is also important to listen even if you are not fascinated by or in agreement with what a person has to say. When it comes to building your network, listening is invaluable, and sometimes you need to listen and nod even if, in your head, you couldn't care less about what someone is saying. Follow the 80-20 rule: listen 80 percent of the time and speak 20 percent. Just being listened to makes other people feel valued and "right." Also, the more you listen—and the less you interrupt—the more information people reveal. Without even uttering a word you can glean important information to help you get ahead.

I first learned this lesson in one of the restaurants where I was a waitress during high school. I always let my customers be right, even if I knew they ordered fettuccini but they insisted they ordered angel hair pasta. I didn't disagree about silly stuff because I had my eye on the long-term goal: a fat tip. My brother, on the other hand, laughs as he remembers his brief time as a waiter at the same restaurant. If the customer said something that pissed him off, he told the customer just that. He was up for a fight and came home ranting and raving about what ridiculous requests people made. As a result, his waitering career lasted all of one day.

I do not want to say that listening means you must always hold your tongue—just that in professional situations, you must pick your battles. If the topic at hand is business related and you disagree with someone's take on a particular strategy or statement, first assess *if* it is appropriate to disagree. If your opinion is based on your particular expertise, if you have credibility to challenge the statement, and if what you are disagreeing with is worth the potential fallout, then it is okay to step in and appropriately flex your professional muscle.

Here's an example of a time I used listening to assist with a project and build a relationship. I was sitting in a meeting with a client who was outlining the tasks that my company needed to deliver. The client was creating dates for completing these tasks without taking into account the necessary development time that my computer programmers needed to put new software features in place. I knew I needed to correct him, but I wanted to ensure he completed his laundry list of features before I reset his expectations. Had I interrupted him midstream, I might not have captured all the information I needed, and it might have even turned into a heated debate. By waiting until he finished, I understood all his concerns and allowed him to feel he had expressed them thoroughly. Then I stated that since I wanted to properly set expectations, he had to understand that we would not be able to commit to his dates but would assess the requirements and get back to him with a realistic deadline. This way, he felt "listened to," felt respected, and knew I was focused on meeting his needs. In the process of planning our schedule, I solidified our relationship because he knew I valued what he had to say.

My point: listen before you speak.

When should you listen and refrain from responding? Say a person you work with is blabbing on and on about the upcoming election, and you could not disagree more with his view on one of the candidates. Let it go! Some women are tempted to disagree for the sheer sake of showing the men they work with that they have a backbone, that they're tough. But you do not always have to boil the ocean. If you get into a heated discussion just to satisfy your ego (something men do too readily in social situations), you'll undermine your original mission. Besides, you don't have to agree with everyone you work with or everyone you meet. Neither must you pressure them to agree with you.

◆ **What it takes:** Listen and respect others' opinions. It's both professional and polite.

Network Outside the Office

When you undertake any type of research, you have to go to different sources to glean the fullest and most accurate picture. And usually, some of the most valuable information—what exciting projects are coming up, what the boss likes and dislikes, which department is about to have layoffs—is not gleaned at formal meetings or in bulleted reports but over sushi and sake at informal gatherings. And usually, the most valuable information is sandwiched between non-business-related topics, such as the latest baseball scores or the progress on your boss's home renovation (which you probably couldn't care less about). You have to get out to get the scoop. Consider it a job requirement.

◆ **What it takes:** Socialize with colleagues and business associates. It's not avoiding work, it is just another way to work.

Don't Rush Home Every Night

The lure of your family, your significant other, and friends is strong at the end of a workday. But I urge you to extend the workday into the evening, even just once or twice a month. A real estate broker in New York City recalls that, in the early days of her career, she forced herself to join male colleagues at after-work baseball games, dinners, even out-of-town excursions. She admits it was easier because she was single: "Other women who were married or in relationships felt compelled to return home right after work. I think I got ahead because I was able to develop relationships that those women missed out on."

You don't have to be part of every outing or industry soirée, but don't fall into a habit of perpetual absenteeism, either.

◆ **What it takes:** Know that sometimes networking infringes on social and personal time. The good news is that networking can be just as fun.

Invite Yourself

Not all outings are invitation only. Sometimes you can—and should—crash the party when you are not invited. Women are likely to consider inviting oneself rude or embarrassing, but the reason people don't invite you along is not always because they don't want you there but that they assume you don't want to come. So set them straight, as this commercial real estate executive did:

My most eye-opening experience was when I invited myself to lunch with a group of men at my real estate firm. They were a bit surprised (as I was new and had never joined them before) but completely welcoming. Did they talk about guy stuff? Sure! But they also gossiped about their kids, their vacations, and some books they read. Most important, they talked about clients, the industry, and the economy. Within seconds they had exchanged information that would have taken me hours to research—and then they were back to their boats, golf scores, etc. But I saw what an advantage they had over me if I had stayed in my office and ate at my desk. After that, I always make it a point to tag along on occasion.

I once had a client who gathered a team together every Wednesday to play pool. For weeks they would come in the office talking about it the next day. Although I was an outside consultant, I didn't think they would mind if I asked to come along, so one afternoon before leaving the office I said, "Can I meet you all there?" The response: "Oh, I didn't know you played pool. Absolutely, meet us there!" While they spent the next day making fun of my lack of pool-playing ability, I had fun, and it strengthened my professional working relationship with the *company*, not just the other (more talented) pool players.

Sometimes you even have to invite yourself to participate in what you consider somewhat boring activities. Keep this in mind: networking is more about the people you are with than the activity itself. At my last job, for example, the company made an effort to have "Matrix and margarita" days. We would go as a group to see the *Matrix* movies when they came out in theaters and then go have drinks together. I confess I hate *The Matrix*, but I knew going to these events was a great way to build relationships with people in the company I didn't know well.

◆ **What it takes:** Stop pouting and invite yourself. (Just be prepared to take up a new sport or sit through a lousy flick.)

Plan Events Yourself

After attending the events you don't like, initiate activities that you do like. I am not talking about planning the office Christmas party or becoming the go-to organizer for every birthday party. But I do suggest that you occasionally initiate an event, be it a last-minute after-work department outing or a more formal young professionals' happy hour. Taking charge and planning a group outing is not a hostessing task but a networking opportunity. (Just be careful not to make hostess a part of your job function.)

◆ **What it takes:** Create networking opportunities for yourself by planning events and inviting people with whom you want to build relationships.

Network from Scratch

Okay, so you are buying into the notion that having a network is not as horrible an idea as you imagined. So how do you start? Initiating your network can be as simple as attending an industry cocktail party, accepting the next lunch invitation, or asking a colleague to a baseball game.

I began building my own professional network during my final year of business school, when I started my job search. Like most soon-to-be graduates, I didn't have many contacts in business, so I had to start from scratch. I kept a meticulous job-hunt notebook and on every page wrote the name of the company I wanted to work for. Every time I sent a letter, made a phone call, or talked to someone, I noted the date, the time, the nature of the correspondence, and next steps. (Type A, personified.)

I didn't know anyone at most of the companies I targeted. But instead of calling the human resources department (like every other graduate in the country was doing), I looked up a company's website on the Internet and found the name of an executive who ran a division that interested me. I would call the individual, only to learn that he or she was not the right person to contact for a job. But inevitably that person (or the assistant, who I treated like gold) gave me the name of another executive to contact. Then, when I contacted *that* executive, I began my letter by name-dropping: "Your colleague so-and-so suggested I contact you." Instant network!

If this all sounds calculated, too bad. That's how it works (and it's how I was able to land the highest salary of anyone in my graduating class!).

One of the companies I wanted to work for after grad school was Sabre—a division of American Airlines' parent company, AMR—which created and tracked electronic travel reservations. During the fall semester, the company had visited the Texas Christian University campus, but I had been busy studying and did not hear about the interviews. My interest was piqued, however, when a fellow student landed a very lucrative job with the company. I decided to target Sabre on my own. Most people would have shrugged their shoulders and lamented, "Well, I missed the formal interview process, so I must have missed my chance." Not me. I decided to approach the company using what little network I already had.

One of my parents' neighbors was an executive at American Airlines, and I called him up and asked if he could tell me whom I might contact regarding a job at Sabre. He was very kind and gave me the names of a few people. Naturally, I began my letters to everyone with my neighbor's name—"Executive Vice President George so-and-so suggested I contact you. . . ." The referral helped separate me from the horde of job seekers and gave me more credibility than some anonymous job applicant. I am sure some people called me back only as a favor to my neighbor, but who cares? Eventually I got to interview with the right people and landed a job as a business analyst.

◆ **What it takes:** Learn that your network can begin where you least expect it (your childhood neighbor, your dentist, your second cousin's roommate); you never know whom other people know. Second, use recognized names as a reference whenever you can. It helps get you in the door. (But it won't keep you there—that's up to you.)

Maintaining Your Network

Having a strong external network takes time—years, in fact. But if you make it a career goal, like having a certain amount of money in the bank by a certain age, it will materialize. I'm getting there, slowly: at age thirty, I'm proud to say that I can go to almost any city, pick up the phone, and find a former business associate, client, or friend to have dinner with. My handheld PC is packed with more than a thousand contacts, everyone from folks I knew in college and graduate school to former colleagues and clients. There are people from large companies such as Accenture, JPMorgan Chase, IBM, and Merrill Lynch, as well as small outfits. There are some people who I have let slip through the cracks over the years, but I do try to at least "touch" people every six months, whether it's a phone call or an e-mail. I also try not to reach out only when I need something; instead, I check in for no particular reason. When someone calls me, I try to call back as quickly as possible. Networking is a two-way street: it may be my time to help someone else out.

◆ **What it takes:** Nurture your network. After all, it is made up of sincere relationships, so don't just call people when you want something. Call just to say hello.

How *Not* to Network

Earlier in this chapter I said the good news about networking is that, at its core, it's about building relationships, something many women do very well: throw a woman into a party full of strangers and within minutes she's laughing with someone whose client's best friend once dated her college roommate's little sister. Throw a guy into the same situation and you'll probably find him nursing a cocktail near the bar with the few people he knows at the party—people he's known since high school.

That said, building relationships at work also requires that you avoid some behaviors that may serve you well socially but do not serve you well professionally.

Don't Pledge the Office Sorority

Women are great at forging fast friendships, which brings us to the bad news: professional relationships are not the same as purely social ones. Yes, you can be friends with people at work, but you are not at the office to find your new best friend or reinvent your social clique. Those who think so often find themselves stuck in a cadre of catty coworkers. And once you become associated with a gaggle of girls, other colleagues may take you less seriously. What's more, cliques are like magnets, and you risk distancing yourself from, or not taking the time to network with, colleagues who can help you excel.

I have worked hard to maintain my individual professional identity. One company I worked for had a group of women who were always referred to as "the marketing girls." While I was a bit envious of their friendship—and I admit they were women I could see myself hanging out with outside the office—I never made an attempt to join their circle. Because of the sorority-like title they earned, I never viewed any of them as anything more than potential girlfriends. I always heard them talking about their weekend parties, the guys they dated, and the upcoming group vacations they had planned. While I'm sure that some of them had the business knowledge to become executive material, I never felt they would make it, because I viewed them all equally. If I did not see them as executive material, I was sure others felt the same way. So while I admit I love to make new friends and at times was sad not to partake in the laughs, I firmly believed that staying outside the sorority was the best way to maintain my independence.

Many people I interviewed have emphasized this important point: surround yourself with the best talent, not your best friend. But that advice is tough to follow once you are ensconced in office friendships. Think of it this way: in grade school gym class, when a girl is asked to pick classmates to be on her team, not only is she likely to choose her best girlfriends first, she will also probably pass over kids who have athletic skill but whom she doesn't like. A boy, on the other hand, immediately picks the fastest kid, the strongest hitter, the best kicker, whether he likes the kid or not. Boys grow up and carry this attitude into the office: the male coworkers I've seen would rather work with a successful salesperson that they're not crazy about than a friend who can't close a deal. The men I've known do not go to work looking to replace their best high school or college buddy. In fact, many purposely pursue work relationships with the strongest players so they can align themselves with success.

Again, it's your choice. If you're at work to create a social network of friends and just to collect a paycheck, you might as well stop reading. But if you are serious about getting what it takes to move up, read on.

◆ **What it takes:** Align yourself with strong players and be wary of social allegiance at work that can hinder your ability to move up.

Avoid the Cattiness Quotient

No matter how close you decide to become with women in your office, there is a force so compelling that it requires all your strength to resist: cattiness. To be catty is to be malicious or spiteful, especially in a subtle way. Catty people talk about petty matters behind their coworkers' backs, spread rumors, and, in general, gossip in a way that serves no purpose other than to make the gossipers feel important and "in the know." In reality, information such as whether the boss got a divorce or how much money the marketing manager makes has no beneficial effect on your career.

Cattiness can flare in almost every office setting. Sure, it is tempting to join in because talking about other people is a way women bond with each other starting in elementary school. But at work, you only have so much energy and there are only so many hours in a single workday. To spend it on fighting losing, petty battles is a huge waste of time and energy. This is something men understand. How many times do you see men lounging around talking about their boss's ugly wife or whispering behind their coworker's back about the stupid statements he made during the client presentation?

Men avoid being catty by stating their complaints and moving on to the next subject, but also by avoiding the secrecy that makes disagreements or differences of opinion more hurtful than they need be. In short, men usually say exactly what they're thinking, and they say it out loud. If a woman wears a ridiculous outfit to work, the women in her department may whisper about it behind her back. If a guy shows up in an ugly tie, a fellow male worker is more likely to walk up to him and say, "What the hell are you wearing?" When a woman says something silly, other women whisper, "I can't believe she said that," over and over for days on end. When a man says something just as ludicrous, his male coworkers are more likely to blurt out, "Do you have your head on straight? That is ridiculous!" Personally, and maybe this is because I am used to such male behavior, I find it incredibly refreshing to say what's on my mind and be done with it. Everyone laughs and moves on. This ability to playfully mock others and even take—and accept— cheap shots face-to-face has benefits in business: it protects you from becoming emotionally tangled in any one issue, and it lets you network among groups of men, because joking with one another is how they communicate.

Because cattiness is, in many ways, so intrinsically female, I often wonder if women even recognize when they're engaged in catty behavior. Ask yourself these two questions:

1. Do you spend more than five minutes talking with a group of coworkers *about* other coworkers?
2. Is the conversation about your coworker not central to a project or the work at hand, but rather something personal and irrelevant to job performance (for example, someone's short skirt, horrible haircut, divorce, or new love interest)?

If you answered yes to the questions above, this is the time you should disregard my statement above about getting out of the office. If you are partaking in this behavior, get back to your desk!

One woman I know has a way to indulge her catty impulses without letting them get the best of her or hurting others. She walks into a trusted colleague's office, shuts the door, prefaces her comment with, "I know this is catty, but . . . ," speaks whatever is on her mind, then walks out of the office. Dirty deed done.

I am not claiming to be immune to cattiness, but I am saying that we should recognize when we are being catty and get back to business. And remember: there is a difference between venting and gossiping. Airing your frustrations to a close colleague takes only a few minutes and can refocus your mind on work. Gossiping with the clique can go on for hours and sap your energy. And if you want to reserve your energy for moving up at work, then cut the cattiness. If all you want is to bring in a paycheck and sabotage your and your colleagues' goals, then by all means gossip away.

Networking with People You Don't Like

If you have finished this chapter and still think networking is a distasteful game, then you probably won't like reading my opinion about dealing with people you do not personally like. Maintaining friendly, respectful relationships with people you dislike is the most political type of networking. Many women will not do it because they don't understand that there is a difference between a friendship and a business relationship. Socially, we can pick and choose with whom we spend our time. At work, we should be less picky. I see too many women let their personal feelings about coworkers interfere with their ability to work productively with them. They believe that, in order to collaborate effectively, they must like their colleagues. And respect them. Forget it. The chances of you liking everyone at your office are minute. The only solution—other than blatantly refusing to work with someone—is to figure out a way to develop a tolerable relationship so you can collaborate and work effectively together.

On *The Apprentice*, one of the other women who didn't care for me personally called me manipulative and criticized me by saying that I used relationships to try to win the game. Of course I used relationships! I may not have liked Omarosa, another contestant, as a friend but I worked well with her and recognized her professional strengths. I may have built solid relationships with the final four candidates, but that's because I knew we needed to work well together to win challenges. Building true friendships at work is nice when it happens, but it is not the goal. Unfortunately, the woman who criticized me, like many women, confused the term *networking* for friendship-making, and once her friends were gone, soon after so was she.

Speak Up

The Rewards of Expressing Yourself

During my first performance review, when I was 22, my boss Tom praised my outspoken nature and willingness to speak up, voice my opinions, and challenge ideas. He warned me, however, to "be mindful of your audience as some managers may not like it when you speak up too assertively." He was right.

Fast-forward about five years to when I was almost fired for speaking my mind. I was at a meeting with a customer and a department head from my company, and my customer was very unhappy with the services this particular department was delivering (or, I should say, not delivering). The department head denied the issues and talked his way out of contractual obligations that his staff had broken. At times, he even scoffed at the client's complaints. I tried to facilitate the conversation without specifically defending either side. However, I truly believed that my company was to blame in many instances and that the department manager's ego was preventing him from hearing my customer's very real concerns.

After the meeting, I confronted my colleague while he was with his subordinates, insisting he misrepresented several situations and should consult with his department to validate the client's concerns.

My hope was that he would return to his office and fix the problems. That, however, is not how he interpreted my comments; all he heard was a junior person challenging his credibility. His ego flared, and he proceeded to call our company's senior management, exclaiming that I should be fired immediately. His team observed his ranting and raving and forewarned me of the uproar. Determined to address the conflict head on, I went to his office to clarify any misunderstandings. He looked up from his desk to acknowledge my presence through the window of his door, but then looked down, shook his head, and refused to talk to me. I left the office for the day and cried on the drive home, remembering the warning I had received years earlier from my first boss, Tom.

I don't tell you this story to stop you from speaking up—after all, speaking up on behalf of yourself, your clients, and your company is critical—but to reinforce how important it is to speak your mind in a manner that, well, won't get you terminated. There are effective and ineffective ways to voice your ideas and opinions. For example, listen before you speak, because if you don't, your message may fall on deaf ears. And don't open your mouth the minute thoughts flood your brain, because unformulated ideas are unimpressive, and sometimes silence is best. And don't plunge headfirst into dialogue with just anyone, because who you talk to matters. Finally, do not speak up about just anything; give voice to too many inconsequential issues and the critical ones may get lost in the shuffle.

When many of us were girls, being loud and noisy was frowned on. We were told speaking up was impolite and unladylike. Meanwhile, the most outspoken and rowdy boys were often the coolest. Perhaps that is why most men I've worked with rarely hesitate to speak their minds. Be it an opinion, a self-interest, a new idea, or an accomplishment, men seem to air their thoughts easily and without angst or apology. Not all their ideas are impressive, and not all men are worthy of the self-promotion they heap on themselves. But that doesn't stop them from speaking.

In the workplace, the traditional keep-quiet rules of girlhood do not apply. Speaking up—highlighting your accomplishments, volunteering ideas before they're asked for, voicing opinions, asking for what you deserve—is critical to moving up.

- Speaking up is how you ensure credit for your own feats
- Speaking up is how you avoid responsibility for others' mistakes
- Speaking up is how you share ideas with people in positions to act on them
- Speaking up is how you show intellect in action
- Speaking up is how you impress superiors and motivate coworkers

Speaking up distinguishes you from others and grows your career. The art of speaking up is knowing how and when to do so.

The Most Important Rule: Listen before You Speak

It might seem odd to begin a chapter about speaking with the topic of listening, but the most effective way to ensure people hear what you say is to hear others *before* you talk. That way you can shape your language to best reach and win over your audience. I cannot emphasize this enough, although as the story at the beginning of this chapter illustrates I have not always shaped my language correctly. Years working as a liaison between my company and clients have taught me that listening carefully is the most important key to speaking up—and in my job, no one is more important to listen to than clients.

For example:

- I listen for *preferences*: if a client makes it clear that he or she is in charge and expects me to follow directions, I'm careful to use more respectful language and not to make major decisions without consulting the client first.
- I listen for *professional style*: if the client is very formal, I do not pepper our conversation with personal anecdotes and colloquial language.
- I listen for *concerns*: if a client has severe budget constraints, I include a detailed breakdown of cost considerations when we discuss new projects.
- I listen for *priorities*: if a client needs to solve a specific business issue before further customizing my company's software, I help him or her focus on that business issue before focusing on customization options.
- I listen for *clues*: if my my client wants to be perceived by his or her boss as the "mastermind" behind an idea (even if it is mine), I make sure not to steal the credit as I know it will benefit my company in the long term.
- I listen for *vision*: ultimately I am the one who must get the client to its destination step by step and I want to make sure I reach the right goal.

In short, I listen carefully and then cater my message, language, and actions to the client's preferences. While you may not work with clients in your particular job role, listening for these types of clues with whomever you interact will help you craft your own messages.

Career coach Susan Murphy told me she is astonished by how many people *don't* listen. Murphy counsels executives in the advertising, architecture, and construction fields and says listening is perhaps the most difficult skill to drill into her (mostly male) clients' minds. "The trouble with men in particular," says Murphy, "is that they're quick to declare themselves experts in a certain area and launch into whatever topic is on their mind with little regard for the interests, expectations, or expertise of the person with whom they're speaking." Women aren't entirely off the hook here: many of us are prone to interrupting and to finishing other people's sentences to prove we already know the answer. But in general, women blab because we're eager to prove ourselves, and men blab because their egos give them free rein. Both sexes can use a lesson on listening.

Listening before you speak serves three purposes.

1. Listening lets you learn and become familiar with your audience so you can fashion your message to meet both your goals.
2. Listening helps you make your audience more comfortable and more receptive to your input.
3. Listening puts you in control because the more familiar you are with someone else's style and preferences, the more you can modify your own style and message to make your point.

Murphy shared with me how she explains the process of effective listening to her clients.

Step 1. When you initiate a meeting, take control of the conversation by saying something like this: "I'd like to talk to you about [insert topic you want to discuss], what are your thoughts?" In one succinct sentence, you've taken control of the conversation by identifying the topic you want to address (rather than letting others hijack the meeting with their agenda) and signaled the others to provide input.

Step 2. Let the other participants talk, and absorb the messages and content with sincere interest—not just polite head nodding. Your goal is to hear everything they say in an effort to understand their viewpoints and perspectives.

Step 3. Probe the person with questions and seek clarification of statements. The more you ask leading questions—"Would you describe your ideal outcome?" or "What is your biggest concern?"— the more you learn about people's specific agendas, biases, and goals. Thus, the better equipped you will be to adjust your language to make your point.

Step 4. Repeat back what a person says. Not word for word, but paraphrased so she knows you understood. Use language such as, "So what you're saying is [insert summary of the statement]" or "Let me be sure I got that." If you acknowledge others' statements instead of steamrolling over them with your ideas, your colleagues will appreciate that you understood where they're coming from and be more receptive when you voice your viewpoint.

By not only hearing but actually listening to what someone else says, you are finally ready to step in and present your own ideas and points of view. If you propose different opinions, preface your statements with phrases such as, "In addition to your idea . . ." or "Another way of thinking about this is . . ." or "A different perspective from yours is. . . ." Acknowledging the other person's stance strengthens your own.

You may think this sounds manipulative, but it is really about using positive influence. Ultimately, listening, knowing, and understanding others helps all participants get what they want without mandate or coercion. You not only have resolution but a stronger relationship. Think about this approach in a non-business scenario. When you go on a date you ask about the other person's background, family, and opinions, right? And if your date claims never to watch television, you don't launch into a retrospective about the 10 seasons of *Friends*.

◆ **What it takes:** Listen before you speak. By being attentive to others' viewpoints first, you can more effectively adapt your message to get what you want.

When to Speak Up

Speak up when you have a thought that *adds* to the dialogue, project, or issue at hand; you owe it to your employer and to your colleagues to share your ideas and opinions on topics where you have experience and expertise. You also owe it to yourself to speak up on behalf of your accomplishments; self-promotion is not about inflating your ego but pointing out to others how your achievements contribute to the greater goals. Unless you speak up, no one may ever know.

Speak Up Where You Have Expertise

Be selective about the content you speak up about. As a general rule, stick to topics in which you have some level of knowledge, not just an opinion. Everyone has an opinion about the company's ad campaign, about product features and pricing, about the color of the office walls. Express your thoughts on everything, and your voice may lose its effectiveness when it really matters. And, most likely, your opinion is most valuable in areas where you have expertise and experience. Unless asked, a financial analyst sitting in a product planning meeting with designers should keep quiet about the new proposed name of a product even if she hates it; she should save her energy for the real reason she's participating: to make sure the budget is acceptable.

Michelle, a principal planner in law firm specializing in land development, exercises this same rule in her line of business. At her company, each member of her team of "good ol' boys" has a specific area of expertise on land development. One person is responsible for zoning, one is responsible for subdivision, one is responsible for site planning, and one is responsible for permits. She says that in their meetings they have established roles and responsibilities and that they respect the others' professions. To keep meetings effective and prevent predominately male "I know it all" egos from interfering with productivity, they have a policy of "You do your part and I do mine." By agreeing to speak up only about their specific fields of knowledge, they make their meetings more effective.

◆ **What it takes:** Speak clearly and with conviction about your area of expertise. Don't tell others how to do their jobs.

Speak Up for the Recognition You Deserve

In an ideal world, your results would speak for themselves. The right people would notice your contributions and recognize you with promotions, praise, and pay. Unfortunately, the modern workplace is far from ideal, and you must learn to speak up about your accomplishments—verbally. In short, learn to brag (perhaps the second *b*-word women fear most). When I say brag, I do not mean in the obnoxious, seventh-grade, I-got-a-gold-star-and-you-didn't sort of way or in a pseudoconfident, "me, me, me" sort of way, but in the subtle, sophisticated businesswoman way to highlight your talents, your results, and your strengths.

Susan Mangiero, founder and managing member of BVA, LLC, a business valuation and litigation support firm, says the key to speaking up about accomplishments and talents is not to come across as self-serving, but group-serving. Mangiero suggests talking about your accomplishments in the context of a group goal. For example, instead of focusing on your expertise, focus on how that expertise benefits the group. When talking to colleagues, say something such as, "Based on my experience with X, I believe that idea will improve Y for the company." And rather than stating your accomplishments directly, emphasize how your accomplishment leads to larger results, "My idea to develop X will improve Y for our company."

When you speak up in a way that combines accomplishments, the "X" part of the equation, with company goals, the "Y," you demonstrate how your skills serve others and not just yourself.

◆ **What it takes:** Remember that results rarely speak for themselves. Promote yourself and your unique expertise with consistency and confidence.

Speak Up about Small Successes

Granted, all achievements are not blockbusters. There are also minor, ongoing accomplishments that you can and should call attention to subtly, such as participation in special projects, deadlines met, progress made.

Sherry Savoia, president of the placement firm Palladium Employment, says that before she owned her own company, she spoke up about her accomplishments by writing a short report or minutes from meetings that she handed to her boss before he left on business trips. Sherry knew her boss routinely used his time in airports and on planes to read and catch up, and she saw a great opportunity to get her minor accomplishments—deadlines met, projects in progress—in front of him. If Sherry had simply said, "Everything's going great, enjoy your trip!" or casually told him what she was up to, he would not have given it the same level of attention.

Another simple way I ensure awareness for small successes is by regularly forwarding e-mails I receive from customers and senior management to my immediate boss. If a customer writes, "Nice work on project X," or if a vice president says, "Great job on presentation Y," I send it on to my boss in a subtle "hey-we're-keeping-the-guns-happy" sort of way.

◆ **What it takes:** Document daily deliverables because it's an understated way to make a statement about your success.

Speak Up About Risks and Problems Before They Escalate

Speaking up about escalating risks and problems can be a stomach-churning endeavor. Still, you must do it. Hiding potentially bad information does not make it go away, and no one appreciates hearing about an issue or problem when it is too late to solve or stop it. Follow this rule: do everything you can to prevent your management from being surprised by unforeseen issues. If a project is off track, even if you are responsible for a major blunder, bring up the concern honestly and confidently.

If you try to tackle issues alone, you may find yourself more alone that you ever intended. Lindsay, an architectural estimator, recalls a past experience:

> *My company was falling behind schedule on numerous projects, and I knew if I did not step in to help, we'd be in big trouble. I didn't want to bother my boss with the problems so I juggled multiple activities outside my job description because I thought it was the right thing to do for my firm. The only problem: my boss had no idea what I was doing every day. I was so busy solving other people's problems that I did not make time to tell him, nor did I see the need. When times got tough and the company had to make staff cuts, I was the first one out the door. The reason? I was an estimator, yet my boss saw little evidence I was*

doing much estimating. Before I could even explain all the crit-
ical time I was spending on problem solving, I got my pink slip
and was escorted out the door.

◆ **What it takes:** Bring issues and risks to the surface to prevent others from being surprised. Always keep management aware of the
good, the bad, and the embarrassing.

How to Speak Up

Perhaps one reason that women cower from expressing opinions
in meetings and in general is that they fear they will be perceived as
wrong or, even worse, stupid. Speaking up is not about being right
but about helping everyone get to the right answer. And that answer is likely a combination of everyone's ideas. If you are concerned about being wrong, or if you only speak when you think
someone will praise you, I challenge you to shift your mentality.
You do not have to be right all the time. Your ultimate goal should
be to exercise your intellect and contribute to the group goal. Of
course, there are optimal ways to speak up.

Be Prepared When You Speak Up

The best ideas surface and important messages are heard when
expressed: a) in a way the recipient is willing to hear with an open
mind; b) in a format that penetrates a this-is-the-way-we've-
always-done-it corporate structure; and c) objectively and professionally, not emotionally.

Passion is important, but we can get so worked up about our
message that we jump too early to communicate it. I have done this
many times: I'll get an idea and run into my boss's office to share it,
but the idea gets buried in my enthusiasm because I have not ex-

pressed the idea clearly, have not articulated its benefits, or have not thought through potential problems. I make no sense whatsoever and get the glazed-eye stare from my boss.

Before you jump into communication:

- Process your thoughts
- Prepare your message
- Validate your points with facts
- Plan your delivery
- Anticipate potential questions and be prepared with answers

Whatever you want to communicate, let your emotions die down and plan your delivery so your boss appreciates your opinion or idea as much as you do.

Planning your message is even more important if you want to get past the gatekeepers of corporate bureaucracy and traditional corporate culture. Habit and egos can prevent new and better ideas from replacing traditional ways of doing business. In addition, people are territorial and bureaucracy gets in the way. But do not let these barriers stop you from speaking up. Carefully plot and execute your attack. Kathleen Thibault, cofounder of Engage Communication, a presentation skills training firm, recalls a previous job where she spoke up and ultimately changed company policy:

> *I never used to speak my mind at work, but barely a year into my sales job at a large training company, my entire sales department was unmotivated. Their commission was basically nonexistent on top of a low base salary, and every day everyone complained to each other about how overworked and underpaid we were. But no one approached the management team. I suggested*

to a coworker that we speak up or nothing would change. Because of the way the company's male-dominated, old-school management team worked, I knew we could not just complain and expect change. Instead, we needed to back conviction with data.

First, we asked ourselves four basic questions: What is the problem? What are the causes of the problem? What are the possible solutions? What is the best possible solution? We spent time answering these questions objectively with other sales reps and wrote out answers to each point in a three-page report—noting, for example, that our commission was lower than the industry average and suggesting that the sales department hire a college intern as a cheap way to reduce administrative work that took time away from selling. We asked our boss for a meeting at which we presented the findings and spoke honestly and confidently. He listened, asked questions, and told us that he would get back to us regarding the requests. I was proud of us but apprehensive, a bit worried I'd put my job on the line.

To our surprise, our boss called us into a meeting two days later to tell us he was doubling the whole team's sales commission! I almost fell off my chair. Later, I found out that he was impressed with the time, thought, and solutions behind our complaints. Plus, he did not know how unhappy the staff was until we told him.

While I'm not advocating that everyone in your office rally together to attempt to bump your pay, Kathleen's approach to properly voicing concerns was very effective. To ensure she was heard, she evaluated her audience, prepared her argument, and spoke professionally about an emotional issue.

◆ **What it takes:** Present ideas seriously if you want them taken seriously.

Share Ideas with the Right People

You have an idea that doesn't seem to be getting the reaction you anticipated. Maybe you have been talking to the wrong people. Rethink your network—whomever you've been talking to—and target decision-makers, people who have the ear of decision-makers, as well as colleagues with reputations for being open-minded. Take an example from Christy Jones, founder of the Internet company pcOrder:

> *As a cofounder of the technology company Trilogy, I was always interested in branching out beyond our core product and creating a computer configuration application, but as Trilogy expanded it became less of a company priority. I did not, however, give up on that vision. In my free time I wrote the business plan, got support from the board, and approached the CEO about heading up an independent company to focus on my solution. The CEO told me that he would support the plan if I was willing to trade in all my previously vested shares to make it happen. I took the risk and created a new company, pcOrder, to sell the application in 1995. pcOrder boomed along with the stock market and the company was worth almost $2 billion at its height.*

◆ **What it takes:** Speak up to the right people to achieve the maximum results.

Do Not Wait Your Turn

Do not be timid about jumping into a discussion during a meeting, especially if you are surrounded by men. If you don't jump in, you may never be heard. Meetings are not like high school classes, where you raise your hand and get called on (or where you keep your head down and pray you don't get called on). Wait your turn and that turn may never come. You must insert yourself into the fray. I can't count how many times an idea has occurred to me and, while I waited for just the right time to break into the conversation, some guy muscled his way in before I knew it and voiced my very thought. But I have learned through the years to jump in confidently when I have something to add.

Just recently, I was participating on a new CNBC evening show with a few confident, outspoken businessmen, including Joe Kernen, Jim Cramer, and Donny Deutsch. If you've seen them in action, you know it's hard to get a word in edgewise with these boisterous guys—they've been trained to talk and are great at making sure their ideas and perspectives are heard loud and clear. I could have patiently sat there in our televised discussion, waiting for a lull in the conversation, but I was pretty sure that the right moment would never come and that I'd hear "It's a wrap" from the producers before I said one word. So the minute the show began, I made a conscious effort to jump in the conversation to share my perspective and one time even had to say something like, "Hey, now, give the lady a little respect. I've got something to add. . . ."

◆ **What it takes:** Confidently insert yourself into the conversation. If you wait too long, you may never have the opportunity.

Stop Apologizing

Trust yourself and have faith in your point of view. I see too many women put an apologetic disclaimer on, or tiptoe around, their opinions: "I don't know if this is right, but . . . ," "I'm no expert . . . ," "Sorry to bother you, but. . . ." Such caveats come out almost automatically. We assume up front that others won't agree with our input; by apologizing, we take their side immediately, scared we'll be judged, be left alone, or come off as stupid. In general, delivering opinions with apprehension makes us sound weak, like we don't trust ourselves.

That said, while I believe you should state your opinion without any preface, you may still feel the need for a verbal launching pad of sorts. Here are some options that will not discount your opinion but provide a nice lead in:

- "I have an idea to share . . ."
- "How about this approach . . ."
- "Add this idea to the mix . . ."
- "I've been thinking about something interesting . . ."
- "Here's an option . . ."

◆ **What it takes:** State your opinions, don't apologize for them.

Rein in the Rambling

I speak up regularly, which is good, but sometimes I tend to ramble. Rambling happens to the most articulate among us. Sometimes we speak without knowing the point we want to make, and we just hope the right message will surface. Other times we keep talking to maintain our platform, out of fear we will be ignored. Another reason we ramble is that we're waiting for physical cues of approval from whomever we are speaking to. There have been times when, until I witnessed some serious head nodding, I felt I needed to go on and on and on. These days, I'm much better at cutting myself off, because I know the consequences: my message gets lost in my gabbing (case in point: my final interview on *The Apprentice*). So I challenge myself, and other guilty parties, to stop talking once the point is made, regardless of the message recipient's body language. If people need clarification, they will ask for it.

◆ **What it takes:** If you hear yourself talking, shut yourself up.

How to Speak Up about Accomplishments

Among the best reasons to speak up is to make sure others are aware of your achievements. While formal performance reviews are the most accepted time to highlight accomplishments, don't wait for your annual review to draw attention to your successes. Throughout the year, your accomplishments should be visible. The trick is doing this without coming off as an approval-seeking, insecure employee.

Stealth Bragging

Weave talk of your accomplishments into natural discourse instead of delivering a canned speech to your manager. My former client at Quadrem, Ian Hollingworth, shared this advice for women in search of recognition: "Be casual and matter-of-fact about sharing accomplishments with superiors. Get your point across quickly, and be thick-skinned about whether or not you get an immediate response." Ian compares selling yourself to product advertising. "Get the billboard up and things will happen; just don't expect people to comment about it every time they walk by." In other words, don't look for approval with every comment, just get your thoughts out there.

Also, do not insert yourself into your description of the accomplishment. Let the results, the company, or colleagues be the subject of the conversation rather than yourself. For example, avoid the word *I*, as in, "I did such a great job . . ." or "Did you notice how I. . . ." And if you do use *I*, aim for a soft reference that does not make you the center of attention. A few examples:

BAD BRAG: "The client loves me!"
GOOD BRAG: "The client has given rave reviews. We have a
    solid relationship."

BAD BRAG: "Can you believe what a great job I did in that
    presentation?"
GOOD BRAG: "The presentation went extremely well. We
    couldn't have asked for more."

BAD BRAG: "This new solution was my idea."
GOOD BRAG: "This solution I've been working on is exactly
    what we need."

◆ **What it takes:** Know that strategic bragging is not an obnoxious, self-centered affair.

Let Others Speak Up for You

You do not have to be the only person who speaks up about yourself. Career coach Susan Murphy suggests subtle ways to ensure others speak up on your behalf. First, tout *their* accomplishments, and inevitably they will tout yours. Take time to tell a colleague's supervisor what an effective presenter or reliable researcher the colleague is, and compliment your colleague in person, when warranted. If you feel someone is doing good work, there's no need to let your feelings remain a mystery to him or her.

Another way to create an environment where others voluntarily promote your strengths is to foster effective communication in general with everyone you work with. This means listening, encouraging others to open up, acknowledging their perspectives, and being approachable and honest. You can still be tough, but as Murphy explains: make other people comfortable, and they will be comfortable enough to acknowledge your worth. Hammer on coworkers, and they will likely withdraw and won't want to give you or others the satisfaction of knowing if you're successful.

My former boss at BetweenMarkets, John Price, has said one of the best ways to be recognized and heard is to have someone else speak up about you. I wholeheartedly agree. Now, we're not suggesting you prod people to whisper in your boss's ear about how amazing you are, but if your work has "impact, and if you have charisma, people will line up to say good things about you," says John. Create strong bonds and solid relationships and people will voluntarily sing your praises. Michelle, the principal planner in a law firm, shares another experience:

> *For more than ten years I have represented real estate developers in the zoning and planning area for retailers, multi-family housing units, and office developments. To that extent, I present our cases to local politicians, environmental interest groups, and neighborhood associations for their approvals. In this male-dominated environment, it is important to exhibit confidence and assertiveness, which is not always easy. Fortunately, I have the unique opportunity to work for an attorney who is extremely supportive and expresses his confidence in me to clients, consultants, and politicians. On several occasions, when we discuss our roles on projects, I have indicated that "I work for him," and he has come back with the comment, "No, actually, I work for her." Coming from a real estate attorney with more than twenty years' experience, that is the ultimate compliment.*

◆ **What it takes:** Develop strong relationships with others so they endorse you, voluntarily.

Keep a Bragging Folder

Our days are so busy, the weeks zip by so fast, that we can easily lose track of our own successes as we leap from one project to the next. The big problem: at performance review time, we scrape together bits and pieces of our accomplishments from memory and aren't able to present a full, accurate picture of our year. Solution to the big problem: keep an ongoing folder of your accomplishments and accolades. Whether a quick note about a sale you closed, a report you drafted, an article that quoted you, or a complimentary client e-mail, the folder organizes all the good news in one place and can be a quick useful reference before a performance review. I spend a lot of time on e-mail, so I actually create an electronic folder of my accomplishments. I save key progress reports along with customer e-mails I'm proud of. (Note: Don't whip the folder out during a review or pop open your laptop to show the boss your long file of e-mail accolades. Keep it as a personal reference to help you speak about your performance.)

At the very least, a bragging folder is a nice little ego boost when you're not feeling so hot. Just open it, page through your accomplishments, and, boom, instant satisfaction—sort of like speaking up to yourself.

◆ **What it takes:** Track your successes now so you can tout them later.

Just Say No

No is that two-letter word women fear to hear and fear to use. We feel compelled to say yes, so people will walk away and think how helpful and nice we are. Well, guess what? Nice is not a word that gets you far in business. No one gets promoted simply because she is nice, no one gets asked to attend executive golf outings because she is nice, no one gets more money because she is nice. No, however, is a different story. While no is painful—it may go against your nature to turn people down or be unable to accommodate them—you must exercise it. No is your friend. No buys you credibility, and no buys you time.

Say No without Uttering the Word

The $250,000 question, of course, is how to say no in a manner that causes the least discomfort and ill will. Murphy suggests that, in addition to saying no, you provide a reason why and, when possible, an alternative. A few more suggestions from a variety of sources follow; mix and match, or adapt what's right for you.

- "I'm focused on other projects right now and won't be able to give yours the attention it deserves."
- "Thanks for thinking of me, but my schedule is already full."
- "Ordinarily I'd love to, but I wouldn't want to take on another project unless I knew I could give 100 percent."
- "What a great assignment, maybe I can suggest someone else."
- "I just don't have time to do that right now—why don't you ask Steve in accounting?"
- "I am currently working on [list your projects]. If you want to hand off one of those projects to someone else so I have more time to complete this new task, I'd be happy to take yours."

And remember, say no with a positive tone of voice and a forthright manner. Don't apologize or ask if saying no is okay; be firm and clear. You'll be respected for it.

◆ **What it takes:** Have faith that saying no does not make you look overloaded or incompetent but rather like a confident, focused businesswoman.

Say No to Assignments That Don't Further Your Career

One of the side effects of being responsible, diligent, and easy to work with is that you get a reputation as such, which means everyone wants to give you work. Sometimes you want to accept, other times you must accept, albeit reluctantly.

Linda, a senior manager at a global consulting firm, has learned that almost everyone at the office has a project you can work on, but most of those projects are not going to help you move up. Says Linda, "Especially when you are driven, you want to do everything well"—but not everything is good for you. Linda has reached a level in her career where she feels comfortable saying no and only chooses projects she deems strategic and challenging, or as she says, "where my heart and mind are aligned." Granted, senior executives have earned the right to say no to requests, but get in the habit early in your career and you will move up more quickly because you will not get bogged down with busy work.

For a while at Commerce One, I had started getting recognition for my work and was being assigned a lot of "special" projects. I was asked to prepare presentation materials. I was asked to scope international customer projects. I was asked to participate on every task force. At first I was quite proud of myself for being recognized as a star player—then I came down to earth and realized I was no star, just an easy target: people knew I would not say no. Eventually I was pulling 80-hour weeks to complete all these assignments to perfection. I had become the go-to girl, but that reputation wasn't getting me anywhere. If anything, I was proving I could not prioritize my time.

One day my boss asked me to manage a large software implementation at our own company, not at a client site. While I recognized the project was aligned with my company's goals, it was not aligned with my professional goals, which included rising to an executive level and working in the field with customers. If I accepted this latest assignment, I limited my opportunities to work with customers. And, because I knew I was capable of doing well on the project, I feared typecasting myself as an internal operations specialist. For the first time in my professional life, I said no to a project assignment. The move felt risky, but after I explained the professional reasons why I did not feel the job was in line with my career path, my boss said he understood. Saying no was also a chance to express my own career intentions, and within a month my boss offered me a better opportunity that fit my own as well as the company's agenda.

When deciding what requests you can rightly turn down, use common sense, balancing your own goals with company goals. You can say no to:

- Work that someone with less experience and talent could easily handle
- Work that does not fall within your job responsibility
- Work that may typecast you into a role that is not aligned with your professional objectives
- Assignments that would not particularly impress the people who have the power to propel your career in the direction you desire
- Busy work and administrative activities that are truly not your job; tasks like booking restaurant reservations and sending overnight-mail packages that an assistant should handle
- Work you would not want to add to your resume
- Work that does not challenge your mind but that consumes your day

Be cognizant of requests made of you, and make sure you are not consistently taking on assignments that are outside your job role and that don't further your career. Once you realize people give you assignments simply because you accept them, and not because you are brilliant, the more comfortable you will be saying no.

I'll cap this section with a word from Jessica, a journalist who has carefully crafted her beat.

> *I want to be known as a serious journalist, and while I don't mind doing nice feature stories, I refuse to do sensationalistic fluff. When I've been asked to do pieces that fall into that category, such as male strip club stories and sex toy stories, I go to my executive producer and rationally voice my concerns with valid reasons as to why I'm uncomfortable with a particular story, and it's always worked! I believe that's why I've been able to spend time in Iraq covering the conflict there, why I am often assigned to cover Washington, D.C. . . . and why you don't see me reporting about smut.*

◆ **What it takes:** The strength to say no to unproductive work.

Say No to Micromanagers

Being micromanaged is an annoying problem for those of us who work well independently and don't need a lot of supervision. You know you're being micromanaged if your boss is constantly coming into your office or looking over your cube wall, if he or she is repeating requests and telling you how to go about the details of your job, or asking for updates for every single task you complete. Don't pull your hair out! There's no need to indulge every pattern your manager sets for the way you work together. Yes, the boss will establish early a preferred tone of communication, but there is actually a crafty way to curtail micromanagement and retrain your boss.

At one of my jobs, there was a high-level executive at the company who had once held my very position. As such, he was the perfect candidate for a micromanager because he knew how to do my job very well but he didn't know me very well. Every day the man flooded my e-mail with inquiries. Is the client satisfied with the latest deliverable? Did you create the agenda for the onsite? Did you update the project plan and communicate the new target delivery dates? Have you solved problems X, Y, and Z yet? Arggh! While I couldn't ignore him, it was not worth my time to give him what he really wanted: detailed e-mails about client feedback, my agenda, the outlines for my projects plans. If the pattern continued I would never get any work done.

To ensure we did not get into a you-say-jump-and-I-jump pattern, I used my behavior to set expectations about how I would work with him. I responded to his e-mails with brief messages that said either yes or no, followed by an invitation such as, "Feel free to drop by my status meeting today at 4 p.m. for a full update." I refused to fully indulge his need for details and instant updates, and over time he either dropped by my status meetings or waited to receive my regularly scheduled progress reports. Without ever explicitly saying no, I eliminated his micromanaging habit (or at least stopped him from micromanaging me).

Another approach that may help get a micromanager out of your office is to ask the person to set aside an hour to review projects. This corrals all nitpicky questions into a set period of time while still treating them seriously. I also use that hour to gain my micromanager's "insight and expertise" about certain topics (stroke the ego, ladies), and sometimes I address areas about which he or she has concerns in excruciating detail. I say excruciating detail because telling people more than they ever wanted to know reinforces your level of understanding, satisfies any concerns about your ability, and deters them from asking again. In one hour you've satisfied the micromanager's need for control with your need for independence.

Micromanaging brings back memories from the final episode of *The Apprentice*, when Bill Rancic's team—Nick, Katrina, and I—accused him of micromanaging us as we prepared for the celebrity golf tournament. Granted, Bill had a lot on the line that day, but we tried to rein in his tendency to micromanage us, so we could do our jobs to the best of our ability. Setting boundaries lets you work more effectively and maybe, just maybe, your good work will help your boss get promoted—or in Bill's case, hired!

◆ **What it takes:** Refuse to cater to micromanagers; establish alternative communication early in the relationship.

Say No to Protect Your Personal Time

There is a great scene in the movie *Office Space* where the lead character is frantically trying to leave the office just before 5 p.m. on a Friday because he knows his boss is going to ask him to work over the weekend. He doesn't escape in time, and sure enough, the boss sticks his head in the guy's cube and tells him to be at work Saturday at 9 a.m., and again on Sunday! I laughed out loud watching this scene because I've definitely been in those shoes too many times.

Look, we all work hard, some of us longer hours than others, and the occasional late night and weekend at the office is to be expected. There are, however, lines you should draw when work inappropriately or unfairly impinges on personal time.

Some people go through their careers with a blanket policy of no weekends at the office; the rest of us choose one at a time. One of the most intense arguments I ever had with a client was over whether my team had to come in and work on a weekend. My client was extremely upset because he had a division in Australia that made a last-minute request to test software over the weekend, and he told me this at about 4 p.m. on a Friday afternoon. Rather than acquiesce and please the customer at all costs, I stated that improper planning on their side didn't justify an emergency on ours. I knew my argument was sound and justified, as the testing was not critical to any deadlines. I asked him to reschedule and stood my ground. While the discussion intensified into a (very) heated debate, my team did not come in, and by Monday the episode had blown over. I am all about jumping through hoops to serve customers when my company has made mistakes, but by establishing boundaries and being willing to say no, I believe you actually boost your level of respect.

◆ **What it takes:** Respect your personal time, and others will, too.

Speak Up to Get the Job You Want

Jobs rarely find you. A recruiter may call, a friend may refer you to a position at her company, but to land the most exciting and lucrative jobs you have to explore. And once you find the job you want, you must speak up.

Don't Wait for an Invitation to Interview
Yes, you can ask for a job that is not available. After working at Sabre for two years, I was not thrilled by my options for career growth. If I wanted to move up I would likely have had to move to back to headquarters in a new city, which I didn't want to at the time. So, I began to research other strong technology organizations where I could work with customers, earn a large salary, and have a greater chance for upward mobility. One such company was right under my nose.

Sabre had recently partnered with a small procurement company called Commerce One, and I was impressed with the start-up's business model, its current and targeted customer base, and the employees I had met. Unfortunately, Commerce One was not hiring. Deterred? No. I quietly researched the names of its regional directors and contacted them by e-mail and a follow-up phone call and simply stated, "My name is Amy Henry and I currently work for your partner, Sabre. I would like to arrange a meeting to speak to you about job opportunities." One manager accepted but cautioned that a meeting might be premature because Commerce One was not hiring until the company landed some new accounts. I didn't care. I just wanted to get face-to-face with the hiring manager. So I hopped on a train from my home in Connecticut to his office in New York City.

During our informational interview, the regional director reiterated that the company was not currently hiring, but he also said that even if they were, I lacked experience in supply chain management, a prerequisite for the job. I jumped up from my chair to make my case. I went to a whiteboard in the office and drew the Sabre business model first and then the Commerce One business model. Then I illustrated the parallels between the two businesses and explained how the two companies had similar customer types in similar industries with similar challenges. He couldn't argue. I essentially convinced him that even without a background in supply chain management, I had the transferable skills be an account manager at Commerce One. I also convinced him that hiring me soon was in his best interest because I had relationships with some of their targeted clients and could help get sales representatives in the door. He agreed, and within a few weeks I had a job offer and, ultimately, a new job. I worked at Commerce One for four years.

Don't confine yourself to traditional job tracks. Many people mistakenly follow industry tradition when it comes to moving up in their careers, simply because, "that's the way it's always been done." Here's how ambitious reporter Jessica fast-forwarded her own career track in journalism:

> *I was working as a reporter in Ardmore, Oklahoma, and after a year it was time to make my first career move. As a reporter, it's common to start in a very small market like Ardmore, and then move to another town—slightly bigger, but still suburban. Only over time do reporters move up to big-city television stations. I decided to be nervy, though, and contact the news director in Oklahoma City, a much larger market. I knew someone who worked there who helped me get the meeting with the news director. I sat down with him and confidently explained why I was qualified to be a reporter in his news department. I asked for the job, and he ultimately hired me. By taking the risk and boldly speaking up, I fast-forwarded a few years on my career track.*

◆ **What it takes:** Don't wait for an employer to find you, and don't assume the employer you find will automatically interpret your value. Articulate how your skills and experience are transferable.

State Your Intentions

You do not need to play hard-to-get during the interview process. This tactic might work in your dating life, but companies want to hire enthusiastic and self-motivated candidates. Don't come off as desperate or annoyingly eager, but do come off as optimistic and confident, as though you know what you want.

At the conclusion of every job interview for a position I really want, I say just that: "I'm really interested in working here." Announcing your intentions shows hunger and confidence without coming off as insecure. Remember, there is a difference between wanting to *leave* your current employer and desiring to *join* another. You don't want the job because you hate your old one; you want the job because you envision a successful future for yourself *at that specific company.* Stating so does not imply you want the job at any salary, however, so be prepared to ask for what you're worth.

I often go one step further. When the interviewer asks if I have any questions, I usually say, "Is there anything about me that concerns you and makes you feel that I am not the right candidate for the job?" This gives me a chance to correct any misunderstandings or respond to any concerns. If such a question seems presumptuous, consider that, by the time you ask that question, the interviewer has a fairly good idea whether or not you are an appropriate fit for the job role. If the person thinks you are, this question won't hurt your chances. If the interviewer thinks you may not be a good fit, then this question gives you one more shot to find out the objections, reaffirm the value you believe you can bring to the organization, and hopefully change the person's opinion.

◆ **What it takes:** If you want the job, make it clear.

Create Your Own Job Description

Changes in your personal life (a spouse is transferred to another city) or personal preferences (you don't like your client) that require changes in your current work setup do not mean you are doomed to lose your job or must find another employer. You can recreate your position at the same company simply by speaking up and asking for what you want. I know women who have asked to change accounts, departments, work out of their home, transfer to another city, switch bosses, and work reduced hours. And most have gotten what they wanted. Too many people assume their employer will reject a proposed modification to the status quo and don't even bother asking. Trust me. If you're a professional with a solid reputation, you'll be surprised at what you can arrange for yourself—if you speak up.

Say your significant other is transferred to another city, which happened to me. I needed to move from Texas to Connecticut but my employer at the time, Sabre, had no job openings. Because I wanted to stay with the company, I got creative. First I reviewed all the company's internal job postings for anything in the New York area. I called the job's contacts and let them know about my skills and background, hoping that they would be impressed enough to let me work remotely in Connecticut. My tactic worked, and eventually I had several jobs from which to choose. By the time I was ready to move back to Texas, I heard about a potential job opening to manage a large engagement in Dallas. I called the regional vice president and asked for the job. In both cases I made my professional life fit my personal life by simply asking. No one came beating down my door to meet my personal needs.

Dawn shares how she asked for and got the job she wanted:

I loved my job as the director of a girls' overnight camp, but after I got married I had to move with my husband to Houston, far from the camp's location. I really wanted to stay with the organization, so I set up a meeting with the camp's senior management and proposed a new job coordinating camp marketing efforts from Houston. Because about 70 percent of the camp's customers lived in Houston, I told my managers that a Houston presence would benefit the camp, and I explained that I was qualified for the role because of my marketing degree and previous marketing work experience. I also emphasized that most of the tasks could be handled remotely, thanks to e-mail, and I agreed to travel to the camp once a week for staff meetings. The camp made me a great offer, and I worked out of my home for several years, until I had my first child. At that point, I negotiated another job shift, with a shorter workday, more flexible hours, and even a raise! Because I had already proven my reli-

ability and strong work ethic, the camp again accommodated my request.

Here's the trick: When you speak up about the job changes you want—whether a relocation or schedule shift—emphasize what's in it for your employer, not what's in it for you. Instead of saying, "I need" or "I want" or "This would make me so happy," address your bosses' concerns before they even have a chance to broach them: Will a job change hurt your performance? Will it cost the company money? Will the customer you are managing or the line of business you support suffer? When you address these issues as part of your request for change, your superiors know that you have taken the time to think through potential problems, and they'll appreciate it. And, if the company risks losing you because you'll be forced to quit if it can't accommodate your request, say so. You'll likely be pleasantly surprised to learn that your company values you enough to honor your request.

◆ **What it takes:** Ask for your ideal job. You just may get it.

When *Not* to Speak Up

There are times when silence is best, and sitting back in observation mode and letting others talk is the best action.

When You First Start Your Job

John Price, a former supervisor of mine, has a sound theory he refers to as "the first month waiting period." John says new employees should spend the first month in observation mode. Not execution mode, not impress everyone mode, and definitely not speak up mode. Listen and absorb the company's culture, learn who the power players are, and study the politics that existed long before you arrived. Then, when you are well versed in your audience, slowly come out of your shell one opinion, one idea, and one achievement at a time. Early silence will win you credibility and respect; the alternative could label you a pompous loudmouth. Your choice.

◆ **What it takes:** Observe and evaluate first, then act later.

Keep Mum about Information You Aren't Ready to Make Public

Be wary of letting too many peers, except truly trusted colleagues, know information that you are not ready to announce to the group, and especially to people in senior management who have the power to act on it. This applies particularly to creative ideas you may have. If you think coworkers are too good-hearted to steal your ideas, consider Casey, a West Texas energy consultant, who worked on a team and prematurely shared a few great ideas about what should be done on a certain project. Everyone was excited about this proposal. But before it could be shared with management, one of her teammates presented the idea all by himself to the partner and willingly took all the credit.

Also, keep mum about job-hunting activity. One friend of mine was casually interviewing with outside headhunters in order to stay on top of potential opportunities. He told a few too many people at work, and someone blabbed to his boss. My friend was soon let go.

When in doubt, err on the side of silence. I believe in a healthy level of paranoia. Your ego may urge you to share your great idea or your job offer with others, but resist until the time is right and until you are ready to face all the consequences. If you don't, you may lose the credit you deserve, or worse, you may lose your job.

◆ **What it takes:** Unless your actions and ideas are everybody's business, keep them to yourself until the timing is right.

When You Can't Talk Your Way out of Mistakes

Have you ever committed such a blunder that no apology, no matter how eloquent or sincere, makes the mistake go away? There will be times when you screw up so royally that the problem simply cannot be fixed, and the only solution, after an initial apology, is to shut your mouth and let time and circumstance erase your blunder from collective memory. Sometimes, you just have to get back to work.

Donna, a former computer industry executive, recalls how not speaking up saved her job:

> I'm known for voicing my opinions. Some time ago, I was at a senior management meeting, and at one evening event I was speaking to some colleagues about a highly debated business position. The chairman had supported one direction, yet I felt it was the wrong approach. I was voicing the rationale for my disapproval to a group of people, when the chairman walked up behind me and overheard my conversation. He interrupted me from behind and basically said, "If you feel that way, then maybe you should leave."
>
> I was speechless.
>
> The next day, he began his keynote address by saying that there was one less chair in the audience because some of us can't get behind the company's direction. Ouch. I knew he was speaking to me. I went to my boss the next day and asked if I should just quit or wait to be fired. He told me that I should do neither. I realized the only way to rebuild my credibility was to shut up and get to work. It was a business decision that many wise minds supported, and it was my job to make it the right decision. So I put my head down and led my organization to make sure that my actions in support of the company spoke louder than words.

My organization was soon meeting and exceeding its financial objectives. A while later, the chairman approached me and said, "You're doing a great job. Let's let bygones be bygones." I think that was his way of saying I was off the hot seat.

In closing, I'll circle back to the personal anecdote I left unfinished at the beginning of the chapter. What happened after I spoke up to the department head? First, I realized that I used the wrong approach when I spoke up. I had not accurately read my audience: someone clearly more motivated by self-image than by fixing a problem. I should also have realized that he did not see me as an ally but as a young woman several rungs below him on the corporate ladder and that I should have approached him without his subordinates present. Then, instead of listing raw facts, I should have presented my perspective in a nonthreatening manner and suggested solutions. The situation could have been a winning one for the client, the department head, and me, but it wasn't. Eventually, someone had to leave the company—but it wasn't me it was the department head. He spoke up, but not about the right things which I discussed in this chapter. He didn't speak up about his expertise, he didn't speak up about his good ideas, he didn't even speak up to alert others to critical issues in his department. Unfortunately, he only chose to speak up to waste his breath on me.

◆ **What it takes:** Speak up with substance.

Step Up

Embrace Challenge, Take Risks

Only minutes after the last episode of *The Apprentice* aired, my dad called me on my mobile phone and said: "So, do you have a job yet?" There was no "Well done, darlin'" or "It's The Donald's loss." Nope. Dad wanted to know whether or not I would soon be employed. He was not being mean or condescending, nor was he ignoring my accomplishments. In his own way, he was being protective of his eldest daughter. Dad wanted to make sure I was safe, and for him, safety has always meant being employed by a stable company. By asking me if I was employed he was reminding me that he worked for the federal government's Bureau of Alcohol, Tobacco, and Firearms for almost thirty years. His mind-set was shaped by my grandmother, who assured her son that government jobs are steady; they guarantee a paycheck every two weeks and never lay anyone off. As a young man, Dad even turned down a private sector job offering three times his government salary. He preferred the long-term stability.

That is the mind-set I grew up under, and the above scenario— Dad worrying whether I would be okay whenever I veered off a traditional course—has played itself out my entire life. He discouraged me from getting my MBA and, instead, encouraged me to continue working. But I went on to the two-year MBA program at

Texas Christian University and, after graduation, doubled my salary. When I asked my dad whether or not I should leave Sabre to work for a new start-up technology company called Commerce One, he cautioned, "Amy, that's a really risky move. There's something to be said about a stable company like Sabre. If I were you, I'd stay where you are." (Secretly, I wondered if he wasn't bummed about losing the flight benefits the family got from Sabre. No more free vacations to Aruba!) After I explained that I would never hit it big if I only took baby steps up the corporate ladder, he joked back, "Fine, then. Do what you want, but don't say I didn't tell you so. I don't even think you really wanted my opinion."

Dad was right. I didn't want his opinion. I wanted his approval. A resounding "Go for it!" would have fueled my confidence to take my first risky professional step: leaving a secure company to ride with a rickety dot.com that would either boom or bust (and if you follow the technology industry, you know it did both).

I do not fault my dad for his warnings, especially because his concern is always out of love. After all, Dad is a truly amazing father who was extremely involved in my life, and we continue to have an incredible, very special relationship. Yet, when I look around at other women, I know that I'm not alone in this so-called daddy's girl equation, which I define as follows:

protective father who desires to keep his daughter safe

+

little girl's desire to please her dad

=

risk-averse woman

Women's relationships with their parents influence decisions into adulthood. Personally, I think the daddy's girl equation has a lot to do with why some women have trouble taking career risks, while most men take risks as a matter of course. As a little girl, I was admonished to "be a good girl" and "be careful" and was told, "we'll take care of you" and "everything will be all right." Meanwhile, my brother, who was only 11 months younger than I, heard, "be strong," "toughen up," "you can do it," and "swing for the fences." (This last one is literal. My brother was drafted out of high school to play professional minor league ball for the Los Angeles Dodgers in lieu of starting college. It would have been interesting to see how my parents would have reacted had their *little girl* tried to pursue professional sports rather than go to college.)

It does not feel good to go against our parents' wishes. Yet, at the end of the day, most parents accept decisions their daughters make with their lives and are often the first to offer a hug if things go awry. They also celebrate our successes—the successes we never would have if we always took Dad's conservative advice and never took a risk. Knowing all this, it's still difficult to tell my dad things I know he will disagree with at the onset.

Christi Blakelock, a partner of an organizational effectiveness firm, the WildWorks Group, is baffled by the fact that women of our generation were socialized to avoid risk, but, in contrast, grew up with the feminist message that women could do anything. To add to the contradiction, we had few if any professional women to model ourselves after. Christi challenged me to name professional female role models from my youth, and I realized that I could not think of one well-known businesswoman who I wanted to be like. If pressured to name someone I admired professionally growing up, I would have to say Madonna. Her rebellious spirit resonated with me as a girl, and I was fascinated by her ability to constantly reinvent herself. Other than Madonna, when I flip through my mental Rolodex of successful professional women I wanted to mirror, I cannot find one.

While I had the best mother I could have asked for—her influence absolutely shaped my values—she did not have a business career and thus was not in a position to advise me about how to take professional risks. All the other women on my street were also stay-at-home moms, and except for my grandmothers, who both worked almost their whole lives—Dee Dee as a bank vice president and Granny as a church office manager—no one personified the successful working woman. At the very least, a professional role model gives a girl confidence in her potential and helps her envision a successful future for herself. But even though I was socialized to avoid risk and had few working women as role models, I somehow grew into an assertive, confident woman who has taught herself to step up.

Now, what do I mean by step up? I mean any proactive behavior that involves taking risks, exceeding minimum job expectations, and seeking out more responsibility. Stepping up has helped me and many other women move up, and I want it to help you as well, even if taking risk and initiative does not come naturally to you. If you choose not to step up (and it is a choice), you may miss out on a working life filled with excitement, challenge, amazing people, self-fulfillment, pride, promotions, and financial rewards.

It's time to step up: you can't be a daddy's girl forever.

Confidence Is Queen

Stepping up requires confidence—self-assurance in our ability to succeed—and that's where many women falter. In short, we confuse confidence with expertise.

Women assume we must be the brightest person in the room, have all the answers, and know a subject cold before we accept a new assignment, apply for a job, or volunteer for a project outside our comfort zone. Whether it's fear of failure, fear of leaving the predictability of a present situation (or fear of letting down Dad), women do not jump into enough new situations. Many of us aren't even comfortable talking about a particular subject unless it's something with which we're completely familiar.

Men? All you have to do is watch the majority of Sunday morning talk shows and cable stations to see them screaming their opinions. You think they really have all the answers? Hardly. They're just not afraid to *act* as if they do. And when it comes to confidence, there's a big difference between men and women: a man knows he does not have to be an expert to speak his mind; a woman thinks she needs a PhD to speak hers.

I am not suggesting that women step into situations—meetings, new jobs, work assignments—completely unprepared or unqualified, but rather that women accept that they not have to be an Einstein to feel confident about trying something new. Knowledge is not a prerequisite for self-assurance. Rather, I believe confidence comes when we trust in our ability to apply existing strengths, trust our ability to learn, and accept that mistakes are likely and okay.

◆ **What it takes:** You can step up and take risks without being an expert in a specific subject area.

Act with Your Future in Mind

Have confidence in the fact that you are capable of great accomplishments not just today but years from now. You do not have to articulate those accomplishments—running a company, writing a book, being a respected boss—just believe that you have the potential to rise higher than your current job. When you believe in your future, you almost automatically act differently in the present. Consider that almost all successful businesspeople started their careers in entry-level positions; yet even at that stage I bet they envisioned more for themselves than their day-to-day jobs entailed.

More specifically: perform for the position you want, not the one you have. For example, even if you start as an administrative assistant at a company, walk into the office thinking, "One day I will have my own administrative assistant." If you're a project manager but your objective is to be a CEO one day, you need to exhibit leadership qualities and strategic vision instead of just focusing on tactical tasks. Sure, your assignment may be something administrative, such as creating project status reports, but always try to keep the bigger picture in mind. For example, if you write the report in a way that connects daily activities to the company's larger goals, such as cost savings, you show others that you understand how even small tasks connect to larger goals.

When you fail to act with your future in mind, you can typecast yourself in a role you have no intention of staying in. Look at actresses who typecast themselves as sweethearts—Julia Roberts, Meg Ryan, Reese Witherspoon. These women are unlikely to play many villains, no matter how much they'd like to do so. (And if ever they do, I would have a hard time buying it.) Many of my managers have actually prevented me from typecasting myself. One boss, Chris, always introduced me to clients by saying, "This is your corporate business manager, Amy. One day I will be working for her." His comment was a tremendous vote of confidence that helped me envision my own future.

◆ **What it takes:** Step up with confidence today by acting with your future in mind.

Own the Moment

The most difficult time to step up and muster confidence is in a stressful moment, those occasional few minutes when all eyes are on you and your entire future seems at stake. In these critical moments, you can either freeze or choose to act.

When I worked at Commerce One, a technology company that helped large corporations build electronic marketplaces to buy and sell products, the economy was booming and the company had more prospective clients than it could handle. Large, multimillion-dollar companies wanted to meet with our sales team. Prospective clients would come into our offices and, hour after hour, someone from our company would speak to them about our various capabilities: the executive vice president of marketing spoke about corporate strategy; the executive vice president of technology would talk about our software and architecture; and the executive vice president of consulting services would talk about how to implement and deploy the software. Because we were swamped with sales opportunities, and numerous sales cycles were unfolding simultaneously, the company desperately needed other employees to jump in and assist with sales presentations.

One day, while I was working at an East Coast customer site, my department's vice president, Andy, called and asked me to talk about Commerce One's consulting process to one of our largest prospects. He not only wanted me to present our project management approach, an area that was my specialty, but other areas as well—the development cycle, training, and supplier connectivity. The proposition was intimidating because the target client was a consortium made up of Compaq, HP, Hitachi, Samsung, and other major technology corporations. I was petrified at the thought of presenting. So much was at stake. Acquiring this high-profile client would give our young company a new level of credibility. If there was any deal Commerce One wanted, this was it. Initially, I thought, "No way!" No way could I stand in front of executives from the world's top technology companies to sell a technology solution. What if the prospective clients asked me a question I could not answer? There I'd be, looking incompetent in front of everyone. The vision got worse: what if I said something that damaged or contradicted the message our salesperson had already positioned and, as a result, I ruined the sales cycle? Then, of course, I'd be blamed as the reason my company lost the big deal, and naturally, I'd get canned.

In my head, we had already lost the sale, and I had lost my job.

Then I pulled myself back to reality. It was a reality in which I was familiar with the material, a reality in which I knew my company well, and a reality in which I was an effective public speaker. It was also a reality in which I believed in myself and was always looking for challenging opportunities to grow. With that reality in mind, I cleared my head of all negative "what if's" and refocused on the positive "what if's."

What if I did a fantastic job and helped close the deal?

What if I impressed 50-plus technology executives, who then wanted me to be in charge of the project?

What if I impressed executives at Commerce One that I did not yet know, and they sent accolades to my management?

I accepted the assignment and took the risk because I recognized this was a new opportunity to shine, and I could visualize myself shining.

The upshot: the company did seal an initial deal thanks to a combination of people's efforts. While I had many sleepless nights and busy, anxiety-filled days preparing for my presentation, my positive "what if's" panned out. I went on to do additional presentations for many large deals, which in turn led to many e-mails and company meetings where I significantly contributed to successful projects and was recognized for my efforts. Because of that one big risk, I went from being just a consultant to a "star consultant," and that year I was named consultant of the year. I went from being a project manager who a few people knew delivered well behind the scenes, to someone who was known companywide as a strong performer.

◆ **What it takes:** Step up with confidence in the moment because a single event can springboard your career. Prepare for it, and envision yourself succeeding.

Expect to Slip Up

So much of what I learned in my twenties is based on what I've done wrong, and I expect that trend to continue into my thirties, forties, and fifties. In short, even as a perfectionist, I assume I will make mistakes. This sounds obvious, but because women tend to be their own harshest critics, anticipating slipups is one way to give ourselves a break.

Abby, a human resources manager at a private company, told me of a recent workplace blunder. Among her job responsibilities, Abby secures visas for company employees who travel internationally for business. A senior-level employee needed to go abroad, but because he was not a United States citizen, a fact she found out about only one day before he was scheduled to fly, he could not get his visa in time for the trip and someone else had to take his place. The costs in airfare changes alone totaled some $7,000. Yes, this was an expensive mistake, but the way Abby carried on I thought she had killed someone! For days she beat herself up over it. A few months later, I asked her how her annual job review went. "I was praised for creating a new medical plan, implementing an employee reward system, and presenting a human resources status review to the entire company." When I asked about fallout from the travel incident, she said it never came up. Yet that mistake was the one thing Abby really recalled from the last few months. Abby knows that she consistently beats herself up more than she congratulates herself. She also recognizes that if a man did the same thing, he'd probably blame the government for its stupid regulations and the employee for not being clear about his citizenship, whereas she blamed herself for not following the rules.

Forgetting the visa was not Abby's biggest mistake. The biggest error was how she handled the incident: she let it sap her confidence. Dealing with mistakes is a big mind game. Once a mistake occurs, no matter who's at fault, we have two choices: relive it and chastise ourselves or forgive ourselves and accept that mistakes happen. The latter perspective lets us keep our confidence intact so we can take future risks. The former can paralyze us with fear.

Slip up, don't beat yourself up, and continue to step up. In the end, successes overshadow mistakes in other people's eyes, even if it's the failures that stick out in our own minds. Keep the big picture in perspective. Thomas Edison said he never looked at anything as a failure, only one step closer to the desired outcome. Because mistakes are learning experiences, realize that you have a long career ahead of you—likely forty years from the time you graduate college. Women in their twenties and thirties tend to forget that they are only at the beginning of a long and varied working life; we will all have many mini-wins and mini-losses in the course of our careers. Look at me: in ten years, being fired on national television will only be one chapter in my story.

◆ **What it takes:** Realize mistakes happen. Expect them, learn from them, and rather than beat yourself up, step up again so you can move on and move up.

How to Operate Outside Your Comfort Zone

There you are: you've volunteered for a big assignment or just stood up at a meeting to pitch a new idea. Everyone is waiting for you to perform, but suddenly you think, "What the %&#*% have I gotten myself into?" You're a bit out of your element, and you start to feel like an imposter and worry everyone will see through the façade of your fabulous Escada suit and realize you're not the bright woman they believe you to be. That's it, girlfriend. This gig is up. It was a nice run while it lasted. It's time to find yourself a husband to support you because there's no way you can do it yourself.

If such self-defeating thoughts ever run through your mind, don't panic. Take a deep breath and use the following tools to help you move forward in times of doubt.

Say "I Don't Know" with a Confident Spin

If faced with a question to which you don't know the answer, don't sweat it. In my experience, I've learned that you build a better reputation by saying, "Great question, let me find out and get back to you." That honest response is not the equivalent of saying "I dunno," bluffing your way into a corner, or returning the question with a blank stare. It's simple—in the middle of the meeting, all you must do is hightail it to your desk, ask the same question to the person who does know the answer, and then return to the meeting with the right information. Instant superstar status! The phrase "Let me get back to you" could possibly be one of the most valuable weapons in my arsenal.

Another easy tactic: ask people to clarify their questions if you're unsure exactly what they mean. Don't fake it, or you run the risk of looking more stupid answering a question you *thought* they asked rather than one they really did. In one memorable interview, a chief financial officer asked me a question about his business that I did not know the answer to. Rather than answer honestly, I rattled on forever with the illusion that the quality of my delivery—confident voice, good eye contact, industry lingo— would outshine the lack of quality of my content. Wrong! The CFO smiled and answered smugly, "You didn't answer the question." He was right, and I was embarrassed. That, ladies, is a real imposter exposed.

One of the smartest salespeople I've ever seen in action was not intelligent per se; he was a former jock who, quite frankly, talked more like a football coach than a polished technology professional. On first impression he was not someone you'd expect to be making multimillion-dollar technology deals, but he closed more than almost anyone at our company. At the same time, this guy probably knew less about the software he was selling than most of his colleagues. What he did know, however, was that his colleague Rinus was the most knowledgeable person when it came to sales engineering, that Jim in marketing was the best person to talk about product features, and that Mark was great at discussing the company's implementation process. In short, this jock knew how to call on the right people to provide the right answers. So when he set up meetings with prospective clients, he'd corral the best possible team of experts into the room and let them do what they did best. Essentially, his team closed the deal for him, while he sat back admiring his genius.

◆ **What it takes:** Be willing to say you don't know the answer. You don't have to be the smartest person in the room; just don't be afraid to ask questions, and know who the smartest people are (and get them into the room with you).

Listen: It Makes You Sound Knowledgeable When You're Not

During moments when we truly know we are in over our heads, it's often best to listen. My first day on the job at Commerce One, I was sent to Eastman Chemical in Kingsport, Tennessee, to work with Eastman's purchasing team for our software implementation. Big problem: I had no clue how Commerce One's product, Buy-Site, actually worked. The client did not know it was my first day on the job, and I was concerned that if I told him, I'd lose credibility. I was also concerned, however, that if spoke too much, I'd risk being an imposter exposed. So I confidently walked onsite and let the client do all the talking; I only addressed general topics about which I could speak with assurance. It was a productive tactic because, in essence, I received free training from a customer who was paying me to consult for him. (Sneaky me.) And, when asked a question I could not adequately answer, I simply pulled a "Great question. Let me get back to you" from my bag of tricks.

Confession: I'm no expert at keeping quiet, because I have a tendency to ramble. If I even start pontificating on a subject that I'm not confident about, I can often talk myself into a black hole of stupidity. I've caught myself doing this repeatedly. Don't fall into my trap. When it doubt, keep your mouth shut, your ears open, and only pipe in when you have something concrete to contribute. And when you do add, keep your statements clear and concise.

◆ **What it takes:** Keep quiet and listen when you really, truly know nothing about the topic at hand (as opposed to just not being an expert in that topic). You will fill in the gaps of your knowledge, and (bonus!) people may assume you are a quiet genius.

Stop Analysis Paralysis and Trust Your Gut

Again, you do not have to have all the answers or be an expert to take on a new position or project. Every job has a learning curve. Men know this and step up confidently to take new challenges. After years of watching men around me step up and take opportunity after opportunity, I have become more confident in my ability to figure things out as I go along, trust my instincts, and take action. After all, that's what you sign up for when you decide to step up.

At one point in my career, I was assigned to help a new company get off the ground. The company, empactHealth.com, was charged with building an electronic marketplace for the healthcare industry so hospitals and healthcare providers could buy certain supplies on-line to reduce costs and improve efficiency. Commerce One's software was the foundation for empactHealth.com's operations. I was sent to Nashville, and for one week I literally sat around a conference table with five of the company's founders and senior executives plotting our business course. I was the only woman among the crew of good ol' country boys (aka older white men who rarely if ever worked side-by-side with a woman) and was the sole point person between these men and my company. They viewed me as someone who could take Commerce One's software product and build an entirely new company, empactHealth.com, around it.

I was in way over my head. While I knew my company's software product well, these executives also expected that I knew how to build a business customized around the software, such as how to formulate a corporate governance structure; how to identify and assign business processes; and how to assess staffing needs. Not only had I never built a company from the ground up before, but there were no models for me to follow, because a company like empactHealth.com did not exist. This enormous undertaking was fraught with unknowns, plus the added pressure of my boss's having told me that, if successful, the empactHealth.com model—essentially, selling our software to build companies— would be a gold mine for Commerce One.

While I was not completely comfortable being the sole contact on behalf of my firm, I had to find the confidence because this was an opportunity for me to display my skills, learn new ones, and make a name for myself. It was better to step up and make a few mistakes than not step up at all. (And I did make a few mistakes, such as underestimating several deadlines.)

Knowing I had to step up, I rallied my confidence in two ways. First, I had faith that my existing project management skills would transfer into this larger role. By definition, project managers are the vehicle for information flow, the central point of intelligence for all the people involved. Project managers are responsible for information retrieval and dissemination. We do not need to know all the information, we just have to know where to get it and how to best communicate it to the right people. So, for example, while I did not need to know the size and number of computers empactHealth.com's datacenter needed, I had to find experts who could figure it out and then had to tell employees back at empactHealth.com. (Multiply that type of problem by one thousand and you understand what keeps a project manager busy all day.) Bottom line: even though this project was much larger in scope than others I had managed, it required skills that I already possessed—information retrieval, relationship management, and effective communication. Knowing this boosted my confidence.

The second way I built up confidence was to trust my gut. It was tempting to analyze every decision and possible action, but given the pace of business at the time there was literally no time to dissect every issue. It was 2000, and our priority was to be "first to market," getting our product into the marketplace as fast as possible before our competitors (rather than waiting until the product was perfect and having no one to sell to). The only alternative to analysis paralysis was to trust my gut and then move, move, move! So, I made a conscious decision to have faith in my choices and not waste time second-guessing myself.

Stepping up on the empactHealth.com project paid off. Within five months we grew empactHealth.com from a start-up company of five employees to a full-functioning operation with more than 75 people. In the years to come, empactHealth.com would merge twice, and today it is part of Global Healthcare Exchange (GHX), which, as of summer 2004, connects more than fourteen hundred hospitals to more than a hundred product and equipment suppliers. GHX is the largest trading exchange in the healthcare industry—

and it all began when a young woman sitting around a conference table with five older male executives stopped her analysis paralysis and stepped up to the challenge.

◆ **What it takes:** Remember you don't have to know everything to step up. Existing skills and instincts transfer to other areas and inform your choices.

Avoid Title Worship

Stepping up also requires that you step up in front of the right people, and often that means talking with senior executives who have more clout than you—or at least a higher title. Being intimidated by power players is a very real obstacle that can prevent women from stepping up or voicing an opinion. Take it from Jessie:

> I always feel stupid in front of my boss. The other day, when I walked into the office in my running shoes, he asked me why I was wearing them. I told him I had power-walked to work. He said, "Do people still power-walk in New York City?" I laughed at his comment but couldn't believe I said something so stupid. I wanted to crawl in a hole. I can never say anything smart in front of the boss. I feel like he thinks I'm just some stupid girl in the office.

Read Jessie's statement again. Did you find anything stupid about it? I didn't. This woman has convinced herself that, no matter what she says, she sounds ridiculous to the "big guy."

My advice? Get over it!

Now, I am not saying certain people won't intimidate you, and you probably don't want to speak to the CEO in the same casual tone with which you talk to the security guards, but letting someone's professional status sap your good ideas, your energy, and your intellect is giving that person way too much power.

My rule: don't let the package be more intimidating than the person. Don't assume by people's titles how smart, knowledgeable, and powerful they are. The trick is to think of people beyond the role they play in the office and, instead, cast them in another one. Remember, every CEO is someone's aunt or uncle. Are you scared of your Aunt Saundra or Uncle Charles? Imagine you met the CEO at a barbeque, wearing khaki shorts and a bad Hawaiian shirt—would you be intimidated? Or this: if you came across the CEO's profile on Match.com, would you give that person the time of day?

Luckily, I rarely feel intimidated by others, even senior executives or CEOs. I may admire, respect, and be in awe of these people and their accomplishments, but those feelings do not stifle my personality. Outside the office we are all just people. If I don't feel as if I can have a beer with the CEO, then I don't want to work for that person.

◆ **What it takes:** To get over intimidation, take your colleagues out of their professional role and plop them in a personal role; they lose a bit of their power in your mind—and you, in turn, become more empowered to step up.

People Will Talk about You: Ignore What They Say

Don't expect everyone to like you. Yes, you want people to be impressed with your skill and competence, but you will not succeed all the time. If you are successful at your job, there will be no shortage of people who label you lucky, an overachiever, or worse, and all too common for women, claim that you brownnosed or slept your way to the top. And if you fail even once, the same people will whisper, "I knew she couldn't hack it."

Your harshest critics are often your peer group; coworkers at your same level. Because they compete with you, your achievements and failures make them reflect on their own performance at work. Thus, their criticism is largely a reflection of how they feel about themselves; it is usually petty and not based on anything you have much control over anyway.

If you base your behavior and self-worth on what a small number of insecure, catty people *may* think of you, you limit your ability to step up and, ultimately, move up.

Men have thicker skins than women when it comes to dealing with criticism, and in this respect I personally am built more like the boys. I took a personality test some time ago, and the psychologist told me the test revealed that I have a somewhat contradictory personality. Professionally, I am a risk-taker and do whatever I want without caring what people think. True. But personally, I want people to like me and tend to be a people-pleaser. Also true.

There is a difference between important criticism, idle criticism, and gossip. Gossip focuses on personal issues, and idle criticism is a professional insult you can ignore. The people who level gossip and idle criticism usually have no interest in helping you excel (as opposed to criticism you receive from your boss at a job review, which is important to acknowledge). After appearing on national television in front of millions of people and reading exaggerated stories and constant critiques of my ability, or lack thereof, I have developed a few philosophies for how to deal with idle criticism— as well as gossip.

First: what other people say about you is none of your business. To an extent it is helpful to know how others view you so you can modify unproductive behavior. Honest critiques can be helpful, but gossip will only hurt your feelings and derail your ambition. Forget about 'em!

Second: if others are talking about you, it is simply because you are interesting. Someone once told me this, and I take some heart in the fact that no one wastes time talking about boring, inconsequential people. When idle criticism flies, perhaps it is because people are just jealous.

Three: retaliation only fuels the fire. Resist the urge. I've learned this through my press experience as well as in the office. Journalists still call me, hoping I will say something about my fellow contestants to get the mud slinging. But when anyone asks me about allegations made about me, I just laugh. Letting insults roll off your back is particularly difficult for women, who often let their hurt feelings and anger dictate their actions. Resist, take the high road, and focus on stepping up rather than lashing out.

Four: rebuild a relationship when you can. While you don't want to participate in immature behavior, you can counter it with mature conversation. If there is some merit to what someone may be saying about you or if you feel you can stop false rumors, go directly to the source and try to discuss the issue. Sometimes a complaint is legitimate, and you know an apology is in order. In other cases, someone's gripe is simply catty behavior, and facing the culprit head on can shock them into shutting up.

Five: there is a difference between being respected and being liked. The personal side of me prefers the latter, but the professional side of me would rather have colleagues and superiors say that I was a smart, competent professional—and a bitch—than the alternative: "She's a nice, lovely person but can't be counted on to get a job done." I don't like not being liked, I just accept it.

◆ **What it takes:** Ignore idle critics and gossips.

Imagine Yourself in the Worst-Case Scenario

When all is said and done, what's the worst that will happen should you take a risk and fail? One way I make myself feel more comfortable about taking risks is to imagine myself in the worst-case scenario should the risky move not pan out.

RISK: I take a job that is unlike anything I have ever done.
WORST CASE: I quit that job or get fired and must move home
    with my parents.

RISK: I bring up a potential obstacle at a meeting.
WORST CASE: Someone says, "You're wrong," and I correct my-
    self.

RISK: I ask to be put on a tough assignment and I just can't
    complete the tasks I'm assigned.
WORST CASE: I don't get a raise or a promotion, or I find my-
    self a bit embarrassed.

◆ **What it takes:** Survive and solve for the worst-case scenario in your mind. Then, stepping up to face a risk becomes a lot less scary.

Counter the Bag Lady Complex

When it comes to supporting oneself financially, many women harbor what private investor and coauthor of *The Old Girls' Network* Kathy Elliott refers to as the "bag lady" complex. Elliott told me that one reason many women do not take risks is that they fear they will wind up in a particularly dreaded worst-case scenario: unmarried, unable to support themselves, and on the street feeding the pigeons.

Guilty as charged!

While I do take risks, it's because I have overcome that exact fear. This may sound crazy, but I've always felt that if I do not have at least a year's worth of living expenses in the bank, I won't be able to pay my bills and could soon be living in a box under a bridge. The good news about this so-called bag lady complex is that my goal of having an ample savings creates a nice financial cushion, which makes the prospect of any worst-case scenario less frightening.

Even if you don't have much savings, you can take a risk if you reduce your living expenses—but not to the extent that you must stand on a street corner holding a "Will Work for Food" sign. A friend of mine went from a $60,000-a-year paycheck to living off student loans when she went back to graduate school. Her daily budget was $11 a day. She still had a social life, she still had her daily coffee (just not from Starbucks), and she was no bag lady. Her short-term financial sacrifice was not as painful as she imagined, and in the long-term she made enough money to pay off her student loans and was happier than ever in her new career.

In order to step up and start her own nonprofit organization, Rachel Muir also stepped down to a less glamorous standard of living. When Rachel founded Girlstart to encourage young women to develop their math, science, and technology skills, she applied for a grant of $500 and opened a credit card account. She did not take a salary for a year, and she ate lots of rice and beans. She even took odd jobs at her apartment building, like sweeping the laundry room floor, so the landlord would reduce her rent. While it took her some years to pay off her credit card debt, it was worth it. Girlstart has served over ten thousand girls and families and has been recognized on *Oprah*, *The Today Show*, and CNN.

◆ **What it takes:** Don't let money be an excuse for not taking a risk. Whether you use your savings, reign in your expenses, or borrow funds from a trusted source, there is always a way to finance a risk.

Tap Your Mentor

One of a mentor's most beneficial roles is to build your confidence and be a confidential sounding board. Anne, an account executive at Procter & Gamble, has a mentor named Michele, whom

Anne describes as a "safe" place to go to air frustrations and to ask questions. Because mentors don't expect you to know everything, just ducking into a mentor's office and sounding off about a particularly daunting situation is helpful. You get your problems off your chest, and your mentor might even have some good advice.

◆ **What it takes:** Mentors can be the secret coach we need to boost our confidence. Use their expertise and friendship to give you perspective so you can step up and move up.

Ways to Step Up

Now that you have mustered the courage and confidence to step up, what exactly should you do? There are many ways to move beyond expectations, discover new skills, challenge yourself, and show your value to the powers that be. Stepping up is a little like giving yourself a promotion, because you give yourself permission to take initiative and make a conscious effort to go beyond the minimum responsibilities your job requires. Once you prove you are ready for more responsibility, you will be in a better position to ask for the real promotion and, of course, the higher salary that comes with it.

Make Decisions Yourself

Sometimes, stepping up requires you to make tough decisions without all the facts or all the approvals. Women in particular tend to seek consensus or permission before taking action, but that process not only makes us look like weak decision-makers, it also wastes time. I often fall into this trap. On *The Apprentice*, when I was the project manager for the Marquis Jet advertising campaign, one of the first mistakes I made was saying to my group, "I am not the only decision-maker; we will make decisions as a team." As a result, we lost valuable time debating whether or not to use the edgy, phallic ad campaign—which we ultimately went with and which won. While leaders do not always make the best choices, Donald Trump definitely respected project managers with conviction who made and stood up for their own decisions.

I once interviewed for a leadership position at a company that had financial difficulties combined with an apathetic and pessimistic staff. The executive interviewing me asked me what would be the first thing I would do if hired. I told him that I would start asking the staff for input about what problems they thought existed in the company and how they thought we could improve the situation. I wanted to earn credibility among the employees before I started reorganizing their lives and snapping orders. After I told the interviewer my plan, I asked him, "Would you hire me for the position?" His response: "No." He said he wanted someone who could make decisions without seeking consent. He wanted a decision-maker who wouldn't look to others to make choices.

My former client, Ian Hollingworth of Quadrem, says that when people step up he expects them to take control and not constantly seek out consent every step of the way. While you don't want to become a maverick who ignores input, you also don't want to look for approval at every turn.

Making decisions yourself is also about standing up for what you believe in, even when everyone else disagrees. Marketing manager Lynne remembers when her company "blindly" killed a software product it was developing for the telecommunications industry, a move with which she strongly disagreed. Rather than accept her company's decision, Lynne scheduled herself to speak in front of the company's executive counsel, presented what she felt was a compelling business case for the product, and challenged the executives to disagree with her opinion. Ultimately, Lynne convinced her superiors to restaff the project, which she says produced a product that not only remains a cornerstone of the company's business but was recognized nationally as one of the industry's top one hundred products.

While it's true that the more experience you have, the easier it is to stand up for and make unpopular choices, it's never too soon to start exercising your decision-making muscle. You'll grow more comfortable with taking responsibility for your actions, you'll be a better business leader, and you'll get credit when your decisions yield positive results (and they will).

◆ **What it takes:** Halt the consensus building and the need for constant approval. Learn to trust yourself.

Act Beyond Your Job Description

Many women I interviewed told me that, in lieu of waiting for a deserved promotion or an explicit order that expands their responsibilities, they promote themselves in order to showcase their talents. In my first months at Sabre, I was responsible for capturing and tracking every time a tour operator used our software to book airline travel so we could bill the operator for each transaction. I'd sit in my cube and diligently track booking trends. It was all analysis, and it grew old and lonely fast. I was known by my colleagues as the Queen of Microsoft Excel. This is why I went to graduate school? To be known for fancy spreadsheets? What had I done? Being the social animal I am, I was anxious to work directly with customers and develop related skills, but I rarely had an opportunity to get out from behind my desk.

One day in a staff meeting, my manager mentioned a request from Mill-Run Tours, a tour company that sold discounted airplane seats to travel agents. Mill-Run Tours wanted to use our company's electronic network to sell seats, but at that time discounted seats were only sold by phone. Everyone agreed it was a great idea, but the travel agents did not have the right software to interact with the airlines and purchase bulk seating, or so-called consolidator fares, on our network. What's more, no product manager—the person who would handle such a project—in the room had the time to investigate what it would take to build the software, how many other companies like Mill-Run Tours needed this distribution solution, and what the potential revenue stream would be.

The wheels in my mind started turning. This was my opportunity to step away from my computer screen and get in front of the customer. Later, at a one-on-one meeting with my boss, I told him that I wanted to talk to Mill-Run Tours and see if its application requirements were something Sabre could develop within our budget. I told him I didn't want Sabre to lose out on a big revenue opportunity (note the sneaky angle, putting the company's priority before my own) and that I would take on the assignment as part of my current job responsibility. My boss said sure, why not? I was volunteering to research a new product at no additional cost. I did it for free in the short term because I saw a long-term payoff. I also sensed it was a rare chance to show off my non-number-crunching skills. After all, no one knew I had the ability to work with customers, and unless I did it on a volunteer basis they might never have given me the chance.

I called and met with the customer to get technical specifications and requirements. I wrote a business plan, created a cost-benefit analysis and a revenue model, and even presented it to upper management for approval. (As chapter seven will explain, this was also a great way to make myself known to senior management.) My work paid off for the company and well as myself: Sabre approved the solution, developed the product, and I was promoted to product manager. My royal reign over Excel had ended.

Don't just take my word for the good that can come from voluntarily taking on extra assignments. Billie Jean is a marketing manager at an engineering company. Here's her story:

My successes have come, and have built over time, because I've identified a need and filled it within my organizations. At one firm, when employee morale was low and unrest was high, I proposed to my boss that we implement an anonymous e-mail suggestion program. He told me to write up my idea in a proposal and present it to senior management. I did, and not only did I get great exposure, the idea was approved. No one told me to do this—I simply felt it would be a good way to improve communication and morale, and, selfishly, I wanted to create the program and run with it. Twelve years later, the company still uses my idea—and I've moved up and on to bigger, better things.

Marketing executive Betsey also stepped up to work outside her explicit responsibilities. She says she is one of the youngest senior vice presidents in her firm because she took it upon herself to step up several times, even though the increased visibility and challenge put her in jeopardy of losing her job.

After my unit's executive creative director was dismissed, everyone expected his direct reports to be fired, too. Rather than sit back and wait to lose my job, I saw myself as a change agent. In the midst of the chaos, I sought ways to make the changes easier for everyone. I went beyond my job's responsibilities and, among other things, voluntarily helped the externally hired manager and, eventually, the new executive creative director implement their vision and mission. I asked people from human resources to technology to suggest ways we could implement the manager's ideas. I met with people in other departments, like technology, to explain the new director's vision, and get the resources he needed, like computers. In the end, the new leaders valued my courage, my chutzpah, and ultimately my advice. I did not lose my job, and I became a trusted advisor to each.

One final note about stepping up: do not let your primary job responsibilities slip when you volunteer for outside assignments, and make sure your direct supervisor is comfortable when you take on extra work or you defeat your ultimate purpose of getting ahead. Stepping up requires extra hours and extra work. There are no shortcuts.

◆ **What it takes:** In addition to doing the job you are assigned, assign yourself a better one. The short-term sacrifice in time and money will pay off.

Pick the High-Profile Assignments

Developing a new product for Mill-Run Tours was a relatively low-profile assignment: a product no one intended to develop or gave much thought to—until it existed. There have also been times, however, when I benefited by stepping up into the spotlight and taking on high-profile projects that, if successful, would catapult me further than if I sat and waited for my next performance review. Managing empactHealth.com was, for example, a high-profile gig.

By definition, high-profile assignments are projects that people in high places are involved with and attend to because the projects' results are directly and tangibly tied to overall company results. These projects may not be any more difficult than lower profile ones, but the payoff can be that much more significant, such as a promotion or increased opportunities. Many times, high-profile jobs are also ones that are expected to fail. These are some of the best assignments to step up and join. If they fail, no one is surprised or holds you accountable. But if you are part of an unexpected success, or for that matter make any improvement whatsoever, you are a hero.

Brandy, an account director in the technology field, remembers one of her own recent successes while employed by a global consulting firm:

> *I was working in the firm's government services division and an*
> *opportunity came up to fix a high-profile customer, a large bank,*
> *which was suing the firm for millions of dollars. The client was*
> *not satisfied with the technology solution and the project was*
> *behind schedule. Even though I had no experience in finance, I*
> *wanted to take over the account and turn it around. To convince*
> *my firm I could do it, I set up meetings with senior managers*
> *and put together a resumé documenting my history delivering*
> *results and making clients happy. They appointed me co-lead of*
> *the project, then sole leader, and I overhauled the account—*
> *replaced the team and modified the software. The client eventu-*
> *ally dropped the suit and signed a new, two-year, $20 million*
> *deal. I became a hero to my firm's executives!*

◆ **What it takes:** Step up to high-profile projects because they can be a better use of your time and have greater impact on your career.

Use Tokenism to Your Advantage

Okay, don't get annoyed at what I'm about to say. Tokenism is when you are the "token" woman, invited to a client meeting, a sales pitch, or an event simply so there will be diversity, or at least the appearance of diversity, in an important meeting. Rather than stewing in your feminist juices at the all-too-obvious discriminatory tactic, take advantage of the situation. As long as you must show up, step up.

Former real estate executive Diane Danielson says that when she was invited to meetings simply as the unspoken token, she accepted: "If my gender got me a spot, I didn't feel bad about it." She just showed off her stuff—her intellect, her opinion, her knowledge—when she attended. She also refused to do "token" tasks, such as taking notes.

I think I worked for BetweenMarkets for a month before I realized I was the only full-time female at the company. I rarely notice when I'm the only woman present, perhaps because I'm so used to working in male-dominated organizations. It did not, however, take the men I worked with that long to notice. Confidence, charm, and friendliness worked to my advantage. One day my boss told me that he was fascinated to see how differently the software developers responded to me versus the man who was formerly in my position. He chuckled, "They never did anything when he asked, but they practically jump out of their seats to help you." Was it because there wasn't enough estrogen in the office? I don't know, and I don't care. I got done what I needed to get done.

◆ **What it takes:** Twist tokenism into an opportunity to step up.

Ask Forgiveness, Not Permission

Many women seek permission and preface their activities with "May I," "Can I," or "Is it okay if I. . . ." Enough already. If you seek permission for every activity, someone might say no. Just show the initiative. Sometimes you just have to move and, after the fact, ask forgiveness for what likely was a successful outcome (in which case you don't need to be forgiven for acting without permission). A sales manager I know recalls her experience working with a top auto company in Detroit.

When a client began working on a new project with our main competitor, my boss told me we had lost the deal and that there was nothing we could do to win it back. He told me to stay away from the competitor's work team and focus on our own project, but I ignored him and started working out of a conference room in the competitor's work space and for five months was the only person from my company working at the competitive client site. My mere presence kept my company on the client's mind, and eventually the client awarded us multimillion-dollar assignments as part of its new project. My boss congratulated me, saying in so many words that I was right and he was wrong.

◆ **What it takes:** Forge ahead. Don't let lack of permission stop you from stepping up.

Dance with Butterflies

Whenever you step up, expect to get butterflies twirling around in your stomach. Expect nervous knots. Expect to sweat. These are all good signs, because when you're worried, it's a signal that you know what you are getting yourself into and that you are smart enough to know where potential problems and challenges lie. Only then can you take appropriate steps to overcome them. Just don't let butterflies and fear of failure stop you from moving up. Don't let anyone, even a protective father, fuel your anxiety.

When I told my dad that I was going to quit my job and dip into my savings to be on a reality television show, the first thing he said to me was: "You're crazy." Of course I was crazy! I was smart enough to know that I was taking a huge risk. But I held my ground: "Dad," I said. "How will I ever know what exciting opportunities may arise if I don't take the chance? You never know. I may have an opportunity to write a book."

Exposed

Sexuality in the Workplace

For a period of several months while at Commerce One, I managed a large project that entailed working closely with a client to build a web-based company as a spin-off. The company's primary investor and customer was Columbia/HCA, the largest healthcare provider in North America. The new web-based company's technology would allow hospitals to buy healthcare supplies more cheaply and more efficiently over the Internet. The client's management team was a cadre of good ol' boys from Nashville, Tennessee; I was the only woman among the group and the sole point of contact between them and Commerce One. For six months I commuted to Nashville and worked twelve-hour days. I interviewed potential candidates for senior-level positions, managed timelines for delivery of multiple projects, and developed programs to educate and train future users in hospitals across the country. I had strong, friendly, and productive relationships with most of the senior executives as well as with the team I managed. During this time, the company grew from five to 75 people (many of whom I had hired) and was soon handling transactions with dozens of hospitals. It was the height of the Internet boom, and you could just see the executives salivating over the prospect of taking the company public and becoming instamillionaires.

One day, an executive said to me, "Amy, I'm so glad you work in our office every day. You make it a joy to come to work." I beamed with pride, assuming that he was referring to my hard work, accomplishments, and professionalism. Then he dropped this bomb: "It's so nice to have great eye candy in the office."

Eye candy.

I had an MBA, a six-figure salary, an impressive resume, not to mention that I'd been working my butt off for this guy and his cronies for the past six months to build *their* company. And, with one comment, he reduced me to a big bowl of Hershey's Kisses.

Needless to say, I was not the least bit flattered. His company was paying 250 bucks an hour for my consulting services, I'd worked incredibly hard to make it successful, and *this* was my reward? Infuriated, I gave him my best "screw you" smile and walked off, quick to turn the corner so as not to give him an extra second to glance at my ass. Disgusting. But I fought back in my own way, by continuing to work diligently and with intellectual rigor, competence, and results.

A few months later, the same executive approached me to go on a very important sales call and lead a demonstration of his product to a prospective customer. Payback time.

When I declined, the look of anxiety and fear that crossed over his face was priceless. Even though he was a senior person, he needed my mind and experience—not my looks—for the sales presentation. I savored the sight of his mounting desperation and waited for him to beg. Then I said, "Why, honey, would you want *me* to attend this important call? I'm just eye candy." With his tail between his legs, he told me I was the best person in the company to demonstrate the technology's functionality. Not exactly an apology, but close enough.

"Thank you," I replied with extreme satisfaction and moved on to another issue. I had made my point.

Although business is an undeniable opportunity for women to exercise their intellect and build financial independence, the modern workplace is not always fair to us. Despite all the progress we have made into the upper echelons of business, women are too often viewed in a physical or sexual context. That's because the people who still have control over the majority of American workplaces—men—can't stop libido and female stereotypes from affecting their behavior at the office. As one of my girlfriends puts it, "It's like all men see is a uterus with lips talking."

A primary reason women can't escape being seen in a sexual light is that sexuality, in its many connotations, exists in the modern workplace. Men and women who work together are often attracted to each other and do engage in relationships that are more than strictly professional. Specifically, there are inevitable gender-related differences, social dynamics, and attitudes that affect how men and women perceive each other and communicate in a business setting. There are men at work who tell dirty sexual jokes and women who flirt and wear sexy clothes.

Some women have misled themselves to think that men are so enlightened that they no longer view women as sexual beings. Psychology professor Margaret Stockdale, of Southern Illinois University, Carbondale, has spent her career studying gender issues in the workplace and says research shows women don't even have to try to be perceived as sexual to be perceived as, say, sexy or flirtatious. Says Stockdale, "Women must be conscious of that fact, and they need to be able to manage it. That is reality."

The modern workplace is not a sexless environment. While *you* may not be talking about sex or thinking about sex, it is important to acknowledge that gender differences and sexual stereotypes exist and then figure out how to do your best work in spite of them—and, as you will see, in some cases, by using them.

Beyond Blond

Before I go further, you should know that I am 5'8", 120 pounds, and have been bleaching my hair blond since sixth grade (I was born a blond and will die a blond). On most days, I wear little makeup—only powder and lip gloss.

I am also confident in my appearance. I do not wear baggy clothes to hide my figure; I do wear clothes that I deem comfortable and flattering. My outfit of choice in my casual workplace, when I am not scheduled for an important meeting, is jeans and high heels. For business meetings and important occasions I wear conservative pantsuits or skirts barely above my knee. (And, should I be appearing on a nationally televised reality show, skirts that barely cover my bootie.)

Here is what else you should know about me: I did not grow up playing with makeup, practicing cheerleading, or gossiping on the telephone about boys. I grew up playing kickball and riding Big Wheels with boys on my street—where I happened to be the only girl. I spent after-school hours playing volleyball or cards with the guys. I spent summers working odd jobs to build my resume and my savings. In college, I studied hard, maintained a high grade point average, and went camping and fishing with the boys. We drank beer (and on one occasion dipped tobacco), and I'd listen and laugh at their dirty jokes. Being in this environment made me comfortable with boys in many ways.

Did I date boys? A couple. Did I flirt with boys? Many.

I have been called charming and tough, friendly and flirtatious, attractive and bitchy, confident and arrogant. And, of course, I have been called eye candy. I have dealt with false rumors and I've been harassed. I have also dated a few men I know through work (one of whom you may know if you watched me on *The Apprentice*).

I tell you all this because you should know the source of what is sure to be a controversial perspective about sexuality in the workplace.

Using Sexuality Does Not Mean Having Sex

First things first: let's define the use of sexuality in the context of this discussion. Sexuality is the condition of being characterized and distinguished by gender, either masculine or feminine. Using one's sexuality does not mean flirting or having sex. That said, women *can* use their feminine-associated traits (some would say sexual traits)—charm, empathy, appearance, confidence, intellect, and ability to listen, nurture, and flatter—to their advantage in the workplace. Katrina Campins, an *Apprentice* contestant and a top real estate agent in Miami, states, "A woman that claims she doesn't use her sex appeal to sell, simply hasn't learned how to use it to her advantage." Okay, so that statement is a bit over the top, but I believe Katrina's point is that women should feel comfortable acting like women—not like men—by using feminine assets to their advantage. Using feminine assets does *not* mean blatantly sporting cleavage or being flirtatious. Using one's sexuality means wearing clothes that flatter your figure and makeup that enhances your features. Using sexuality also means donning a warm smile, exuding charm, and caring about colleagues—all the things that many women naturally do.

When you look good you tend to feel good and act more confident. That said, good looks and charm alone won't earn you respect. Being attractive and friendly allows you to start with a positive impression, but if you don't back up your appearance and sparkling personality with brains and business savvy, colleagues will be much more likely to label you a dumb blond. Physical and intellectual confidence is a powerful combination in business. Every woman in technology sales I have ever met (and there are not many) is not only extremely attractive but also well respected and successful. That's because, when they open their mouths, these women are tough and smart. Robin, automotive sector sales executive and a previous colleague of mine, is a perfect example. By combining her physical and mental confidence, Robin is consistently ranked among the top sales representatives in her company. She puts it frankly:

> *Let's face it, it's not about flaunting sexuality, but it is about being well groomed; first impressions last a long time. Once you have built a relationship with a customer, appearances will take a backseat and the quality of customer service you deliver will ultimately separate the great professionals from the mediocre—but you can't discount the importance of first impressions.*

As for me, do I get asked to attend sales presentations for my looks alone? No. I'm asked because I confidently stand in front of a room full of executives and sell multimillion-dollar software and services, while answering people's questions intelligently, with hard facts. I also make people more comfortable by being conversational and joking around.

I'm going to say it again to make sure we are clear: using sexuality in the workplace does not mean having sex. It means combining your brains, education, and expertise with feminine traits such as charm, empathy, attractive features, a nurturing nature, and intuition. As Heidi Singer wrote in a *New York Post* article in January

2004, speaking about how modern women have learned to embrace rather than shun their sexuality, ". . . there's a big difference between showing your legs and, well, spreading them." I wholeheartedly agree.

The Reality of the Modern Workplace

An associate of mine recently recalled an occasion when she was presenting a report in an internal meeting to a group of male colleagues and one piped in, "I didn't know you had a body like that." The fact that she was wearing a conservative outfit is almost immaterial. (And I guarantee that even if men don't say something like that out loud, they are saying it to each other or thinking it to themselves.) So unless we want to work in 100 percent female work environments, we need to deal with some unpleasant realities in the workplace.

Men Too Often Misinterpret Female Behavior

Stockdale shared with me a study she and her colleagues conducted in which they videotaped scenarios of both men and women going through an orientation session with a supervisor. When Stockdale showed the tapes to viewers, men saw the women on the tapes as more flirtatious, sexy, and seductive than the women viewers did. Stockdale says that men tend to view women as sexual objects and they filter women's behavior through that lens.

Based on my own experiences, I agree. When an attractive woman is friendly with a male colleague, people say she's flirting. When a man is friendly with a male colleague, people say he's just being friendly or networking (or at the very worst, brownnosing). Here we are, engaging in the same behavior as men, yet we are flirts. How do you define flirtation? Well, when I picture a woman flirting, I see a big smile, lots of giggles, batting eyelashes, and a turn of the head at an unnatural side-angle, as if posing for a picture. Do I do that in the workplace? No, give me a break. And neither do you.

But even if you have no other intention than establishing a professional relationship with a male colleague, your behavior might be interpreted as something other than professional. However you act, it is safe to assume a man may interpret it in a sexual way that you did not intend. Not all men will do this, but be prepared for sexual perceptions to get in the way of your attempts to move up. A former real estate professional told me about a female colleague who asked a male client to dinner after a big presentation only to have him reply, "I can't. I'm married." Not only did he flatter himself by erroneously assuming the woman had more in mind, he undercut her professionalism.

Being misinterpreted as sexy is an unfortunate circumstance that naturally endowed, big-breasted women have come to understand firsthand (although unfortunately, I'm not one of them). If such a woman wears anything less than a muumuu to hide every curve, many people, mostly men, fixate on her chest. A friend of mine who eventually had a breast reduction recalls that her breasts were discussed by boys in school and, later, by men she worked with. Even when she had no cleavage in sight, many men saw her breasts and thought, "Sex!" Her fault? Hardly. Unfortunately, such sexual misinterpretations have professional consequences: the more a woman is seen in a sexy light, the more her respect in the office may be endangered. Says Stockdale, "When women are seen as sexual beings, they get knocked down a peg or two" in the minds of others. That means that the more you exhibit workplace behavior that has the potential to be perceived in a sexual context—from big breasts to short skirts—the more you have to counteract misperception with confidence, intelligence, and the ability to deliver business results that take you *up* a peg or two.

I'll cap off this point with one of my most memorable stories as a woman in business. When I was a project manager at Commerce One, I participated in the most grueling sales cycle I have ever experienced. A prospective client invited Commerce One and its two largest competitors, Oracle and Ariba, to spend a week at the Ritz-Carlton Hotel in Pasadena, California, in a final effort to vie for a multimillion-dollar contract to provide the company's technical infrastructure. This was no luxury vacation. Our team worked incessantly, each of us focusing on our given areas of expertise; I was brought in for my implementation and project management experience. Each day for five days, the prospective client would call us and say something like, "Come to the conference room in one hour and tell us about your supplier software solution," and we'd scurry to put together a presentation that addressed their specific question. I was not the lead salesperson, but there were many times when, during a presentation, the sales leader looked at me with eyes that said, "I don't know the answer, take over!" And so I'd get up and address the question. This went on for five days—more hazing ritual than sales pitch—and in the end we won the account.

Flash forward several years later. The prospect had become a large client, and one night when our team was out to dinner, we were recalling the marathon sales cycle, and my client said to me, "That's when you earned the nickname, 'The Distracter.'" I had never heard this term before. When I inquired further, he confessed that everyone involved in the evaluation process thought the only reason I was on the sales team was so my appearance would distract the potential client from any faults in Commerce One's software application. "But," he went on to say, "we were all surprised. You really knew your stuff."

◆ **What it takes:** Be aware of what men may be thinking, but focus on showing off your nonphysical assets—your intelligence, your experience, your ideas.

Men Can and Do Talk about Sex at Work

Think the modern man is so enlightened? Think again. Recently, I attended an invitation-only dinner for wealthy individuals and Wall Street investors (note: I was neither) to hear a well-known and respected businessperson speak. I was one of maybe ten women out of about 150 people in the dining room. During the speaker's opening remarks he told several jokes. One was about a man who approaches his wife and says, "Honey, we need to cut back on expenses. If you would just learn to cook we could fire the chef." The wife's reply: "Honey, if you would just learn to make love we could fire the gardener." The speaker also peppered his speech with sexual references: mentioning penis envy and, at one point, comparing a company's backward-thinking tactics to "going back to holding hands" (after having sex, of course). The men in the room laughed at every reference. And I laughed, too. Personally, I did not feel offended even though I didn't think the sexual references were appropriate.

A woman, however, could never have told the same joke without putting herself in a very unprofessional light. The reality: men can and do make sexual and other inappropriate references in the context of work, and their reputations among other men are not weakened.

Case in point: a female executive at a large technology consulting firm in Dallas once told me a story about how she was sitting in a meeting with male executives, and for hours she listened to them talk and swear, tell tasteless jokes, and cuss like sailors. When she attempted to be part of the conversation and piped in with a remark that included the word *crap*, the room fell silent. The men couldn't believe she said something so vulgar.

Fair and equal standards? No. But it's reality in many work-places.

This raises the question: if men talk about sex regularly, when should a woman cry tasteless or inappropriate? My response: let tasteless comments pass, but call men out on offensive behavior. What's the difference? Well, it's relative to every woman. I person-ally have a high tolerance for tasteless male behavior because I have had so many male friends. At the dinner, for example, if I'd stood up and declared myself insulted by the speaker's comments, I would have been lying. Also, the action would likely have severed relationships with several potential business contacts. When it comes to tasteless comments, I prefer to gloss over them with a laugh (or silence) and spend my energy on the work at hand. But if you truly feel offended by a man's behavior or consistent com-ments, and if they compromise your ability to work or move up at work, then it could be time to tell him in a single succinct phrase and serious tone, "That is completely inappropriate."

◆ **What it takes:** Realize that men can often make sexual references at work without repercussion. You might not have the same freedom.

Women—Especially Attractive Ones—Are a Walking Target for Work Gossip

I was recently in Manhattan for business and had dinner with Donald Trump's apprentice, Bill Rancic, and two other people we both knew. The day before, a friend said to me, "Don't you worry that if you go to dinner with Bill people will see you and spread the word that you're dating?" I told her that I realized people may talk, but what was I supposed to do, not see my friend? Or, alternatively, hide out in my hotel and order room service? (Yeah, right. All I needed was someone to see us coming in or out of a hotel together and I'd be in for real nightmare.)

Sure enough, a few days after the friendly meal, which was capped off by hugging everyone goodbye, I returned home to Austin only to get an e-mail from a stranger in Boston who told me he heard on the radio that I had a new boyfriend, "Bill the Builder." Less than an hour later, several reporters from national magazines called me to know if what they read in a Manhattan gossip column was true: that I was "canoodling" with Bill over sushi (and even if we were it was no one's business).

It gets more annoying. A few days later, I went to speak at an annual luncheon for a group of accountants, and a reporter from *People* magazine showed up. The event's organizers were very excited that *People* wanted to cover a story on accounting. While I did not want to burst their bubble, I highly doubted the celebrity-infused weekly magazine was interested in balance sheets. Sure enough, they asked to interview me, and instead of inquiring about the subject of my speech—my professional background and business philosophy—they asked me about my love life.

Once public, a working woman's personal life overshadows her business life. This is more true for women than for men. What's more, your life at work is actually an edited version of your full life, just as a television show is an edited version of hours and hours of raw footage. People see a slice of the "juiciest" part of your life and fixate on that. After I was fired on *The Apprentice*, I hoped that people would comment on the contributions I made to my teams—how I negotiated the golf club, secured big advertisements for the rickshaws, and led the all-women's team to victory during the Marquis Jet advertising task. But the main question people always asked was some version of, "So, tell me about Nick. Are you dating?" (For curious minds, yes, we went out a couple of times but decided to remain friends. Nick has asked me, however, to communicate that he is very available and looking for a beautiful, intelligent woman to help mend his broken heart.)

Granted, your personal life may not be exposed in tabloids across the country, but you can be sure it will be exposed in the office and potentially spread throughout your organization—even if it's not true. You can either go to great lengths to conceal your personal life and never be seen in public with anyone other than family or learn to ignore what people say about you.

◆ **What it takes:** Be aware that even a glimpse a of woman's personal life in the office can overshadow her professional life.

The Good News: Gender Stereotypes Can Sometimes Be Used to Your Advantage

Just by showing up to work or walking into a room, other people will form an opinion about your professional status and your level of competence. More often than not, women in business are assumed to hold less authority than they do and to be less competent than they are. This is unfortunate and slowly changing, but in the meantime women can use such stereotypes to their advantage by catching others off guard. I love this story from Meredith, a trial lawyer, because it shows how, instead of wasting energy being offended at others' preconceived notions about her, Meredith uses those erroneous assumptions to gain an advantage over opposing counsel:

Litigation is still dominated by men, and if I am among the first people to arrive at a deposition, I am invariably mistaken for the court reporter. This used to annoy me, but now I choose to consider it a compliment to my youth and beauty. In addition, witnesses are sometimes unprepared to have a younger woman questioning them, and as a result, they tend to be somewhat less defensive toward me as compared to male counsel. I say, if my age and gender permit me to sneak up on them, so much the better for my clients.

There is a widely known tendency for men to view female colleagues in stereotypically female roles such as nurturer, caregiver, and lover, and some men automatically cast female colleagues into roles that, as men, they are most familiar with: mother, wife, mistress, older sister, younger sister, daughter, girl next door, and so forth. Personally, I am often typecast as the girl next door. Lynne, a marketing manager, often gets dealt the daughter card. She has accepted this fate and does what she can to work it to her advantage in business.

I am usually very sweet and diplomatic, and I must have a very innocent face or something because there have been numerous occasions where the sh*t hits the fan and although I am involved, I am the only one that doesn't get yelled at or demoralized in front of a group. I really think some of it has to do with the fact I manage people and relationships at work really well, but I have to admit a portion has to do with my being a relatively young woman in the workplace and men thinking of me of their daughter. I've had managers that have sent me to deliver bad news to executives or customers because they say no one will yell at me. Actually, I like that because I can use this role to my advantage to get unique opportunities that I would not otherwise receive.

◆ **What it takes:** Rather than rant and rave about stereotypes, figure out how to use such assumptions to your advantage.

The Consequences of the Two *D*'s: Dress and Dating

Dress and dating are two *d*'s that both have the potential to establish and sometimes magnify a woman's identity in the workplace. I am referring to how you dress at work and whether you date someone at work. More than for men, a woman's choice of clothing and her personal life draw attention from colleagues. And more than men, women are at risk of that attention being negative.

I will not say that I've never worn a short skirt with open-toed heels to the office (because I have). And I will not say that I have never dated someone I've worked with (because, as I've mentioned, I have). What I will say is that there are consequences to such behavior, and you must be aware of and prepared to deal with the fallout.

Should you choose to dress a bit daringly at the office or choose to date someone you work with, know this:

1. Keep your competency out front. Your primary message should always be that you are a hardworking, professional, and intelligent businessperson.
2. There can be negative consequences—for example, your credibility may be undermined because attention is drawn away from your business skills—so be prepared to deal with them.

The Consequences of Showing Too Much Skin

Let's deal with dress first. Revealing clothing may get you the attention you desire at a bar, but at work it distracts others from your mind, your intellect, your hard work, your business acumen. Whether you intend it to or not, stereotypically sexy attire—a super-short skirt, a low-cut blouse, a tight turtleneck, four-inch heels—communicate sex. Conservative clothing, on the other hand, does not distract because it does not say much of anything.

I do not think you should dress for a convent. Just bear in mind that the consequence of even remotely sexy clothing is that you can't control how others interpret it. Jamie, a consultant I used to work with (who is also a dead ringer for the gorgeous actress Denise

Richards), is one of the most professionally dressed women I know. At work, she always wore conservative suits, closed-toe shoes, and skirts below the knee. Yet the first time I went out with her after a large business conference in New Orleans, she was dolled up in her weekend evening attire with a sexy tank, micro-mini, and high-heeled sandals. Why? Well, she is a hottie, so why not flaunt it? When it's time for a night on the town, she looks sexy and definitely has all eyes on her. But at work she doesn't want to distract people from her intellect. If Jamie wore sexy clothes at work, she knows that some male coworkers might come knocking on her hotel room door with more than business on their minds. (This has in fact happened to her, despite her conservative armor.)

Women aren't much better when it comes to judging other women. They see a female coworker dressed in way they deem sexy and, automatically, they assume she is a bimbo who is trying to use her sexuality instead of her brains to get ahead at work as well as a disappointment to the women's movement. That's a lot of anger and negative energy for a piece of fabric to unleash at the office.

This book is no place for a diatribe on the history of female clothing and professional attire. And, to be honest, I am not the ideal candidate to speak about wardrobe. If anything, I err on the side of dressing too casually at work, but theoretically I believe women should dress for the job they want, not the job they have.

The one time I did step outside of professional attire (literally) to pose in *FHM* (*For Him Magazine*) in lingerie, I paid a big price and I regret it (and not just because my dad can't handle his friends kidding him about seeing his daughter in lace). I am a skilled, dedicated professional, and posing in lingerie is not the best way to put that professional foot forward. But in the moment of the photo shoot, despite the women's agreeing beforehand with each other not to pose in anything too revealing, the music and the cocktails got the best of us, and eventually, we were proudly posing in our panties. Not a great decision. I took a lot of heat—from professional women, journalists, and other media. But what really bothered me, and ultimately caused me to regret the shoot, was an e-mail I received from a mother accusing me of not being a good role model for her daughter or other young women. You know what? She was right. I had been portrayed as a businesswoman on television, and sex symbol was not an image I wanted to associate with that part of my life. Posing in lingerie may have conveyed to a ten-year-old girl that sexiness is a helpful way for a woman to move up in business. Do I want young women to know that looks matter in business? Yes. Do I want women to understand the value of staying fit and well-groomed so they look and feel their best? Absolutely! Do I want them to think they must show off their cans to get ahead? Of course not. But do I think posing hurt my credibility in business? No. I'm smart and hardworking, and the minute people talk to me, I win their credibility and respect back . . . if it was ever lost in the first place.

The point regarding dress, then, is twofold: dress in ways in which you feel you perform best, and dress for the impression you want to make on your audience. If that means wearing an Ally McBeal miniskirt to a sales presentation, just be ready to deal with a distracted audience and to know your product cold.

There are other ways that dress can help you be true to your femininity without strutting around in lingerie or sporting the latest push-up bra under a V-neck sweater at work. Billie Jean, a marketing director at an engineering company, works mostly with men: "As one of the few senior women I often stand out without even doing anything!" In an effort not to draw attention to herself any more than she already does, Billie Jean dresses conservatively—with one safe exception. "I wear great shoes," she says. "I may have on the most conservative black suit and blouse, but if you look down, I likely have on a pair of killer heels. It gets noticed on occasion, but most important it feels like my little secret commitment to maintaining my own brand of femininity in a tough male environment."

◆ **What it takes:** Choose your clothes wisely. Dress has great potential to magnify stereotypical forces that already work against women.

The Consequences of Dating a Coworker

Now it's time to address the second d: dating. You've heard the saying, "Don't mix business with pleasure." Well I say, "Give me a break." Not because I advocate dating colleagues, but because I know it is often inevitable.

Choose not to date a colleague and you sidestep a myriad of sticky issues and potential problems in the workplace. But you also may miss an opportunity for a great relationship. I am a realist, and a pat no-dating rule in today's day and age is just not realistic. People spend a lot of time at the office, and colleagues are often the people we interact with most frequently and with whom we have the most in common.

For a woman, however, dating someone at work can distract people from thinking of you as a business professional, and it can distract you from the work at hand. And although men can often date a coworker without having people criticize them for it (not fair, but true), when women mix business with pleasure, our reputations, in many cases, can and will be tarnished. I'm not saying don't date, but weigh the consequences.

Even if you think it's a harmless fling and won't mentally affect your performance at work, your man may think differently. This is the scenario I've seen unfold, time and time again: romance ends, man gets promoted, woman leaves company. Sometimes she chooses to leave, other times she is asked to go. Here's what happened to Ellen:

I had a terrific career as a pharmaceutical sales rep and was quickly moving up the organization. Then I met Glenn, a charming, intelligent, attractive—yet attached—executive of my company. Although he was married, he pursued me and convinced me his marriage was over. I believed him. We began dating, attempting to hide our relationship from the company, but eventually it ended badly. I didn't really think it would affect my career, but within two weeks of our breakup, I received notice from the company that I was being let go for performance reasons. I lost my job because I dated the wrong person.

◆ **What it takes:** Don't ban dating at work, but evaluate the consequences first. Sometimes they can be more dire than the rewards.

Ways to Avoid Temptation

Male coworkers are easy targets for dating because we have such easy access to them. Day in, day out, they are all around us. But I believe that, in most cases, the healthiest, most successful relationships are with people who have nothing to do with one's industry or profession. If all you have in common with a colleague is a body of knowledge (you both know the formula for calculating annual rate of return), industry gossip (you know which company is filing Chapter 11), and coworkers (you can only talk about your boss's incompetence so many times), then your romance won't last and is probably not worth the consequences.

There are ways to avoid temptation: take off your "work goggles." Similar to beer goggles, work goggles make men at the office seem smarter, more attractive, and more irresistible than they are outside the office. Remove the goggles by getting together with someone in a nonwork setting and talking about nonwork things. Very likely, the object of your desire shrivels into someone you would, ordinarily, not want to date. A former colleague of mine has a policy that she does not talk about work after work, no matter who she is dating. It's a great philosophy. On dates, you don't talk about business, you talk about life. And it's a great way to see if there's a genuine interest in your coworker beyond his image at work.

A final thought: if you feel you absolutely, positively cannot control yourself from being tempted by coworkers but still want to avoid the nasty complications, work in or transfer to an office staffed with men you are absolutely, positively not attracted to. In other words, ask to work on the fat-ugly-short-guy floor.

◆ **What it takes:** Don't fall prey to false attractions. Sometimes you think you like a colleague more than you would if you knew him outside an office's faux social setting.

Manage the Relationship Before It Manages You

Okay, so you met a guy at work that you think you could marry—or at least have a great time with for more than a week. In some cases, workplace relationships do pan out. In Austin, technology company Trilogy is known for hiring the top talent from the top schools around the country. What happens when you put hundreds of smart, intelligent, attractive twentysomethings in an office together to work around the clock? In Trilogy's case, a lot of successful relationships, and not just businesswise. The company's former director of recruiting, Jeff Daniel, who was responsible for hiring, jokes that he has served as matchmaker for hundreds of employees.

In the course of writing this book, I spoke to many women who met their spouses at work. One, Fern Reiss, a chief executive of Expertizing.com, a public relations consulting firm, says she spent two years avoiding a dating relationship at work because she thought people might question her professionalism. "Then I gave up and married the guy. It will be fifteen years this fall, and we have three kids. So much for professionalism." When Fern and her now-husband, then coworker, started to date, however, they were "unbelievably discreet." They never arrived at or left the office together, they never socialized with people they worked with, and they even treated each other differently at work. "When we finally got engaged and announced it, many people were completely taken aback because they didn't even realize we knew each other!"

LouAnn, a director of business development, is also married to a former coworker and says, "Don't ever let people know you are dating." She and her husband did not leak the information until they were engaged, at which time they sat down with their managers and said, point-blank, that they were getting married and that the relationship would not affect their work. Says LouAnn, "Our philosophy was, once we were committed to each other, to be up front and honest so no one questioned our commitment to the job." Before that, however, they went to great lengths to hide the relationship; LouAnn even took a male friend to the holiday party.

I am not suggesting you will meet your soulmate at the office, for I have not. However, numerous women, who have all had successful relationships blossom out of office romances, contributed to these collective theories about how best to manage a workplace relationship:

- Do not date people in your immediate chain of command, either above or below you. In short, if you report to them or they report to you, don't date them.
- When you first start seeing someone, do not tell anyone at the office about the relationship. Do not talk about it, not even to your closest work friends.
- You and the person you are dating should agree that you will not act any way other than professionally toward each

other at the office or in front of colleagues, even when everyone goes out for a drink after work.

- You and the person you are dating should collectively decide how to address your relationship should someone ask whether you two are dating. Are you going to acknowledge it or deny it? If you choose to deny it, say "no" and change the subject, or if you acknowledge it, say "yes" and change the subject. You do not owe anyone an explanation except, perhaps, a supervisor.

- If the relationship gets to a serious stage—the two of you are dating exclusively, engaged, or living together—tell your boss you are dating a coworker and make it clear that it will not interfere with your work. Speaking directly with superiors prevents them from questioning your commitment to your job should they hear rumors. Brevity is key. You do not owe your boss any other explanation nor do you have to answer any questions about the relationship.

That said, no matter how hard you try to keep a relationship discreet or acknowledge it appropriately—and regardless of whether it's a fling or a serious thing—it is safe to expect that you and your love life will be the topic of office gossip, period. It's human nature, and some people thrive on knowing others' private affairs. My advice: before you agree to have drinks with someone or meet him for dinner, make sure you are really prepared to deal with the consequences. Have this chat with yourself *before* your first cocktail:

- Can you handle people gossiping about you?
- Can you deal with colleagues discussing something other than your professional performance?
- Will you become distracted at work by your romance?

- If you continue to date, will your career, reputation, or concentration suffer because others will become more interested in your relationship than your work?
- If you break up, will your career, reputation, or concentration suffer because you either become obsessed with bumping into or avoiding your ex?
- If things go bad, could you lose your job? And is the person in a position to thwart your progress?

◆ **What it takes:** If you ultimately decide to engage in an interoffice relationship, keep quiet about it. Just because you date a colleague does not mean everyone must know.

What You're up Against: The Male Psyche

When it comes to making decisions about dating, dress, and even dealing with and overcoming stereotypes, it helps to know a bit about the male psyche. After all, it is the male mind, with its stereotypes, assumptions, and overriding interests, that causes women to jump through so many of these hoops at the office, right? Your chances of success at work will be heightened if you know your audience.

When it comes to understanding the men you work with, Belle Rose Ragins, a University of Wisconsin-Milwaukee professor who has studied gender and leadership, puts it well: "If you were traveling to another country, you would study the culture and the climate; you would figure out how to translate the language and the customs." In many ways, she says, gender is similar to culture. Men and women have different values and norms, and for women intent on working well with men, it behooves them to know what language men speak, both the verbal and nonverbal cues. Many women already do this. A 1998 study of high-ranking women conducted by Ragins and colleagues at Catalyst, a research organization, found that 96 percent of women said it was critical or very important to develop a style men are comfortable with. This does not mean you must become a man. "Just because you figure out how to act in Ethiopia does not mean you become Ethiopian," says Ragins. In other words, you don't have to give up your femininity to work in the land of men.

By familiarizing yourself with your male colleagues' backgrounds, communication styles, and interests, you'll not only find common ground but get a handle on how to effectively interact with them.

Men Have Sex on the Brain

Most men won't openly admit what I am about to say, but they know it's true: at some point, men think about the women they work with in sexual terms. Sometimes it will be the first thing on their minds, other times it will be a fleeting thought they quickly dismiss. Some men will want to date you, others will imagine sleeping with you. Once you acknowledge this, you can prepare for it and counter it. For example, just being aware that there is a possibility that even the most unassuming male colleague will see you in a sexual light, in addition to a professional one, can affect your behavior.

Jennifer, a public relations executive, was at her first job out of college when an always friendly and much older male colleague invited her to dinner to, he said, "welcome her to the office." He was as old as Jennifer's father, and it never even occurred to her that the colleague had intentions that were other than professional. Flash forward to after dinner in the car ride home when the man's hand landed on her leg. "I was shocked, disgusted, and felt like a naïve idiot for not seeing it coming." Yes, Jennifer was naïve. Had she been aware that even a man three times her age could cross professional boundaries and hit on her, she could have prepared by, perhaps, declining the dinner invitation, opting instead to invite him to lunch with a group of other people.

While we can't change the way men think, there are subtle tactics to recast, or focus, their view of you from the personal to the professional:

- If you go to dinner or an event, go with a mixed group of men and women. To entertain clients, one businesswoman gets four tickets to a basketball game and invites other colleagues instead of engaging in a one-on-one dinner.
- Opt for a business lunch instead of dinner. It is less ambiguous, has a definite endpoint (everyone has to get back to the office), and there is less chance alcohol or romantic lighting will put anyone in the mood.
- Invite male colleagues to bring their wives or significant others to business social events and express your desire to meet them. It helps demonstrate that you are not interested in the men romantically, just as colleagues and friends.
- If you are in a relationship, make it clear you are taken. A retired female executive once told me she had people introduce her as "Mrs." before she spoke to an audience of men. It can help take the sex thing off the table so the men focus on her presentation, rather than other things, during the first five minutes of her speech.
- At the very least, don't kid yourself. Men don't leave their libido at home, so don't leave your common sense there, either.

Another method to prevent male colleagues from getting the wrong idea about your intentions is to subtly shift small behaviors. You need not defend yourself in the extreme, such as wearing a potato sack to work to avoid being looked at as anything other than a professional, or filing a lawsuit every time you get slapped with a not-so-professional comment. We can still be ourselves, but there is a fine line between sexy and sophisticated. Learn how to walk it. A few suggestions from some sophisticated women:

SEXY: wearing a slinky top to the office because you're going out for drinks after work

SOPHISTICATED: wearing a slinky top to the office under a blazer—and keeping the blazer on all day

SEXY: applying makeup or fixing nail polish at your desk or in a meeting

SOPHISTICATED: applying makeup or fixing nail polish in the restroom

SEXY: e-mailing your boss an invitation to dinner

SOPHISTICATED: e-mailing your boss an invitation to lunch and noting three topics related to your projects or department you want to discuss

SEXY: listening to a dirty joke and then cracking your own dirty jokes with "the boys" for the next half-hour

SOPHISTICATED: listening to a dirty joke, laughing, and then changing the subject to something more appropriate or politely leaving the room

SEXY: asking how your colleague is getting along with his wife or girlfriend

SOPHISTICATED: asking your colleague about his kids or siblings

SEXY: inquiring of a male colleague if he has been working out because he looks good

SOPHISTICATED: inquiring how a male colleague's golf game is improving

To get away from all the serious talk for a moment, sometimes sexy can be a woman's silver bullet, although few women can pull this one off. I can't resist sharing this hilarious e-mail I received from Kim, a vice president at a technology company. Warning: don't try this at work, but laugh about it at home.

Don't ever use your sexuality at work, as it will tarnish your reputation and become exaggerated as others retell stories about you. Having said that, let me tell you a story about how I once used my sexuality:

I had just quit one of my first postcollege jobs, and the company kept making more sophisticated offers to convince me to stay. But my mind was made up, and I really wanted the other job. Nonetheless, it was awkward for me to keep turning down my company's offers. Finally, they took one last shot: my boss told me the company president was going to meet with me and offer me a full scholarship to an MBA program, including paid time off to go to school, if I stayed at the company. It was an incredible offer, and I asked my future husband for advice on how to say no to the president without burning a bridge. He suggested I wear a low-cut blouse and tight skirt, as the president was known to be a ladies' man and, thus, would be so distracted that the meeting would be cake. I thought he was nuts, and just to prove my point I walked into work the next day in a tight, low-cut black number. The president was a bumbling idiot in our meeting. I was completely shocked! It worked!

I never pulled that stunt again. . . . I like my meetings to be coherent.

◆ **What it takes:** Be aware that men think about sex more readily than most women, and then you can you better prepare for and prevent potential miscommunications.

Give 'Em Something to Talk About . . . or Not

Socializing professionally with men can be tricky for some women. For me, building a friendly relationship with male colleagues is a no-brainer. It just happens naturally. For others, I know, navigating social situations outside work can be less comfortable. You want to get beyond work and establish a more personal relationship without taking it to a sexual or awkward level.

This is where listening and communication skills pay off bigtime. Ask them questions and listen to their answers. Mainly, you can't always talk to men the same way you talk to women because women tend to talk more about their emotions and how they feel about things. With men, you can and should focus on the tangibles. Here are some tips for social topics that build the right type of relationships.

Family and Hobbies: Talking about his or your family—children, vacations, house renovations—is an acceptable conversation topic. I remember that one guy has three children, that another likes to ride his motorcycle to work and likes to scuba dive. I ask about these interests, and check in. Not only am I sincerely interested in other people, but it takes our relationship to a more personal level without getting *too* personal or invasive.

Sports: Sports is another great neutral subject because most men talk about it regularly. You either like sports or you don't, and you can either converse about sports or you can't. If you are absolutely, positively not a sports person, it couldn't hurt to skim the sports pages so you know, for example, that when people are talking about the Final Four they aren't referring to the last four contestants on *The Bachelor* or *American Idol*. Brushing up on sport basics also helps ensure you don't blurt out something so ridiculous that it becomes a running joke.

Himself: Men love flattery and to talk about themselves. It is their weak spot. But some forms of flattery will get you farther, professionally, than others. My general rule: stroke a man's ego safely by focusing on content, not generalities.

> FLIRTY FLATTERY: "You're so smart."
> SAFE FLATTERY: "That is a great idea."
>
> FLIRTY FLATTERY: "You look great in your golf attire, those
> workouts are really paying off."
> SAFE FLATTERY: "Nice swing! You're lessons are paying off."
>
> FLIRTY FLATTERY: "That shirt looks great. It really shows off
> your eyes."
> SAFE FLATTERY: "That's a great shirt. I'd like to buy one for
> my boyfriend/husband. Where did you get it?"

◆ **What it takes:** To build relationships with men at work by talking about more than business, focus on family, sports, and, by all means, the man himself.

The Best Men to Work With

Talent and professionalism aside, some men are simply better, or easier, to work with than others, and I agree with Ragins who says that a lot about a man's ability to work with women depends on whether he grew up, or has spent significant time with, working women. Ragins suggests that the best men for women to work with are those who meet one or more of the following criteria:

- men who have working wives whose jobs are on par with their husbands' in terms of status
- men who were raised by mothers who worked outside the home
- men who have sisters; those with older sisters are used to having strong women around
- men with daughters, especially daughters in the workforce

The trend is obvious: men who have been exposed to business-women are more familiar with us, less intimidated, and more likely to make the workplace an environment where we can excel.

The Bottom Line

People interpret sexuality in the workplace in many different ways, and women must recognize that their behavior can easily be misinterpreted. To avoid unintended consequences, be aware of the very real gender stereotypes and differences that exist, and realize that you cannot behave the same way as male counterparts.

Personally, I have cultivated a high threshold for immature behavior. And because I spent so much time with boys growing up, it takes a lot to offend me. Incessant foul language, lewd sexual jokes, and commenting about my "sex appeal" over my intellectual contributions are a few places where I draw the line and make it clearly known that the behavior is unacceptable to me. Wherever you draw your own line, know you can be true to your values without getting up on your soapbox and declaring, *"Do not undermine my mind, for I am a professional woman!"*

When I feel offended or annoyed with inappropriate behavior at work, one of my favorite tools to let a man know that he has crossed my line is humor, especially a dash of cynicism and wit. I leave you with this story: in graduate school I was a member of the

Educational Investment Fund, a million-dollar-plus fund managed by a team of mostly men. During one meeting, a colleague snidely remarked, "So, Amy, how does it feel to be the token woman?" While I was tempted to throw my spiral notebook at him and even deliver a lecture, I simply smiled and said, "So, Sean, how does it feel to be the token bald man?" He laughed, but quickly shut up and walked away. In one fell verbal swoop I let him know I was offended, and instead of allowing him to make me feel inferior or insecure as woman, I taught him that I do not factor gender into my confidence or competence, and neither should he. I have nothing against bald men, I just picked a trait that I felt would be his most vulnerable. Thanks to my women's intuition, I was right.

Money, Money, Money, Money

Get What You Are Worth

The Apprentice was not the first time I sold lemonade on a street corner. If you watched the show, you know that the first task Donald Trump charged the two teams of job applicants to do was sell lemonade in Manhattan. After the episode aired, my mom reminded me that at age six I "ran the most successful lemonade stand every summer" in Arlington, Texas. Okay, so that's a proud mother talking. But to hear Mom retell it I was quite the little businesswoman: I'd set up my stand on a busy street corner (location, location, location) when people were coming home from work and "employ" two kids from the neighborhood to help me. I also had my younger brother running back and forth from the stand to our house, refilling pitchers. As Mom remembers it, I was the only person allowed to handle the money.

That last fact does not surprise me. Even at age six I was driven by the dollar—not spending it, but making and saving it. Yet as a little girl I did not want to spend what I made on fancy clothes or toys. In fact, when I did spend my money, it was a huge deal. My first big purchase was a $35 teal vinyl Liz Claiborne purse that I proceeded to leave on a public bus during a family vacation. For days I was distraught not so much at losing the pretty purse but at losing the *expensive* purse.

I recount my childhood obsession with money because how I was brought up to feel about money has everything to do with how much I make, save, and spend as an adult. The same is true for women everywhere. Perhaps you make a huge salary and save every penny, or perhaps you make a modest income and spend most of it. Maybe you make a lot and spend a lot, or earn a little and save it all. The question to ask yourself is, "Why?" For example, I remain a fanatical saver because I was brought up to associate money with security and independence (and to this day, if I do not have enough money in the bank to cover at least one year's worth of living expenses I fear I won't be able to pay my bills). I think my father compounded my saving tendency; he offered to match every dollar I earned with fifty cents as long as I put all the money in savings. I actually became more of a saver than my father every imagined and took it to extremes. Don't laugh (okay, laugh), but as a girl my favorite activity on Sunday before church was to clip coupons from the newspaper. I got this idea from my grandmothers, because my parents were not coupon clippers. (What coupons, you ask, could possibly interest a teenage girl? For one, restaurants. Instead of eating lunch at the school cafeteria, a few friends and I would pile into my red, four-door Ford Escort—a former rental car my dad bought at auction—and drive to whichever fast food place took my two-for-one coupon. And these were my wild days.)

Yet, in the past, when it came to *making* money, I did not have as much control. I wanted money and expected to work for it, but I was not sure how to get the most I could, so for I while I didn't.

While you and I may have different financial attitudes and behaviors, understanding why you feel the way you do about money can help you take more control over how much you earn. And I want you to earn every dollar you are worth.

Daddy's Working Girl

If you are like many women, you are not making as much money as you could. Most likely, you were not socialized to feel that it was okay or "ladylike" to ask for money, and today you are too scared, uncomfortable, inexperienced, or insecure—pick your fatal financial flaw—to tell your employer (or prospective employer) that you want and deserve a higher salary.

You can, however, shed childhood feelings that manifest themselves as adult inhibitions and bad financial habits. It took me a while to learn how to negotiate for more money or to ask for a raise, which is ironic because as a girl I looked for moneymaking opportunities every chance I got. I landed my first "corporate" job for $20 a night, plus commissions, selling programs at Arlington Stadium, the then-home of the Texas Rangers. For every program I sold over my quota I made a quarter in commission. With so much at stake I was not shy about hawking programs, and some nights I'd come home with double my wage in commissions and tips alone. The following summer I worked the front desk at an athletic club for $4.25 an hour. The work was steady, but something bothered me: there was no upside, no way I could exceed my base salary unless I worked extra hours. And while I got some bizarre thrill from making $2 extra an hour with overtime pay, from then on, I only looked for jobs that paid commissions and bonuses, where the upside was large.

My most formative early working experience was waitressing, because waitresses worked for tips and I could control how much money I made, which meant I could maximize my income. Tips were reflective of my performance. My ability to juggle multiple tables, serve each customer well, and up-sell expensive menu items only made me richer! While money was not all I loved about waitressing—I also thrived on the pace, the multitasking, and forming relationships with customers—I would not have been as happy at a job where my salary was capped. Even at such a young age I liked being in control of my financial future.

Before I went to college I had saved $5,000, and my father encouraged me to invest it in the stock market. Because he was teaching me the value of investing as a source of income and as an alternative to spending, he promised to repay me any money I lost. I researched and picked a stock myself. My choice was Home Depot. It was 1991, and even without being a financial whiz I could see that Home Depot's stores were booming and, I believed, destined to grow. They did, and by my senior year of college I took my earnings and indulged in a teal Honda Accord. Practical and mildly extravagant—essentially, the adult equivalent of a $35 teal Liz Claiborne purse.

I received my MBA in the mid-1990s and set my professional sights on the tech industry, not because I had some fascination with computers or the Internet but because that was where the money was most plentiful. In contrast, many of my female friends went to work in industries where they felt a personal connection. For example, my sister the fashionista went to work for fashion house Coach, my college roommate took a job as a director of the summer camp she attended since age six, and my best friend from high school, to fulfill her dream of being a television reporter, took a reporting job in a small Oklahoma town for a mere $12,000 a year. While others did what they loved, I followed a love of money—mainly, I think, because making it had become a way of life for me. The more I had in the bank, the better I felt about my career and myself.

One of the reasons I was money-hungry was because money made me independent—my stash of cash was a constant source of financial independence, and independence was important to me. At a young age I watched the mother of a friend divorce after some twenty years of marriage and struggle to pay her bills. What's more, another friend's father died, and the family was forced to sell their home while the mother returned to teaching and a much lower standard of living. It was horrible to see two women lose everything overnight, through no fault of their own. I thought it was the worst thing that could possibly happen to a woman, and these situations impressed on me the importance of being self-sustaining.

When I entered the workforce and officially became responsible for my own financial well-being, my ability to support myself now had real consequences. I was now in full control, or so I thought.

Making Money in the Real World: Wanting It Is Not Enough

As much as I wanted to make money, and as much as I had worked in the past, I was not familiar with or prepared for the art of negotiating salaries and raises. This is a very common problem among women because we are taught that asking for money is rude or greedy, and we do not always believe we are worth the money we want to ask for. Leslie Grossman, a co-founder of the Women's Leadership Exchange, an organization that teaches female entrepreneurs about finance so they can grow their businesses, says women more often than men think that if they simply follow a career path they're passionate about, "the money will come," as if magically, cash will sprout in their wallets. The reality is that money comes to those who strategically and proactively pursue it. Whether that means negotiating a starting salary, asking for a raise, or sticking to a profitable business plan, getting the compensation you deserve is the result of conscious effort and self-confidence.

Unfortunately, unlike men, we as women tend to feel incredibly uncomfortable, almost wrong, when it comes to requesting money on behalf of ourselves. That phenomenon may contribute to why women still make about 77 cents to every dollar a man brings in. If a man's starting salary out of college is $30,000, and you start at 77 percent of his salary, then assuming you both receive the same annual 4 percent bump, by the time you both retire at age 65 the man has made some $750,000 more than you. Now does that pay gap sound insignificant?

◆ **What it takes:** Overcome apprehension when it comes to asking for money. Intangible feelings of uneasiness have very tangible financial consequences.

What You Need Is Not What You Are Worth

Here's another mental trap women get caught in: we think of salary in terms of what we *need* instead of what we are *worth*. First, what we need is relative. There was a year in graduate school when I lived off subsidized school loans and some savings. Despite daily expenses and a house payment, I survived just fine off about $12,000 a year, and I never felt needy. Granted, my meals out were at fast-food restaurants rather than upscale steak houses, but I did not need much to get by. Yet, do you think that after I got my MBA I asked for a $12,000 salary because that's all I "needed"? No way! A smart, hardworking, diligent professional is clearly worth more than she needs.

Donna, a retired computer industry executive, recalls how she made that same mistake of confusing need with worth when she started her career:

> *I remember when I got my first job offer of $8,600 back in the late 1960s. The salary was way more than I ever needed, and I almost felt guilty. After all, it was $2,000 more per year than my father ever made in his life, and I was only 21 years old. Immediately after I started working, I learned that a male col-*

league at my same level, doing the same job, was making more than $9,000 a year. When I asked my boss why this peer was making more than I was, my boss responded: "He needs to support his family, you only need to support yourself." At the time, I believed him. I didn't need the same salary even though I was worth it. I was so naïve.

◆ **What it takes:** Know that when you think only about what you need, you will never get what you're worth.

You're Worth More Than You Think

It is not easy to put a monetary amount on our time spent, our talent, our skill, and our results. I cannot tell you how much you should be paid at your job—but I can tell you that, most likely, you are not being paid enough. Or rather, you are worth more than you think.

Not only are women more likely than men to undervalue their professional worth for the reasons described above, such as fear of sounding greedy, but women tend to approach work differently than men: we are grateful for opportunities and tend to let money fall by the wayside, like icing on the cake, a bonus. For example, we are so thrilled to work with people we like, or to be employed by an impressive organization, or to have a flexible schedule, or to get paid for doing tasks that we enjoy that we do not make the effort or even realize that we can seek out more pay. Happiness at work is great, but you can be happy *and* paid well.

My first memory of learning how to value my work—although at the time I was unaware that was what I was doing—is of my 10-year-old self, deciding to be a baby-sitter. Always the saleswoman, I sat down at the kitchen table and, with paper and markers, made fliers to distribute to parents in our neighborhood. I proudly showed the fliers to Dad: "Baby-sitter for hire—$1 an hour—call Amy," and he gave me my first lesson in valuing my services. "You know, Amy, I bet you could make $2 an hour." While I was a bit hesitant—two bucks an hour seemed so high that people might say no—I was also excited at the prospect of making that much money. I crossed out the $1 and replaced it with $2, and set out distributing the flier door to door. Within a few weeks, I had a handful of regular customers.

I was so happy at the prospect of baby-sitting and doing a grownup's job that I came up with my own fee rather than figuring out what the market would bear. Dad was right. I could get more if I just asked.

Perhaps you've hesitated to ask for more money because you fear someone will say no and rescind the job offer, or the job you have. But remember this: you, and not the buyer (aka a future employer), should price your services. If you were shopping for a pair of shoes you'd want to pay the lowest price possible. But when you find a pair of shoes you love, you're willing to pay as much as the price tag says. When it comes to work, if you do not ask for the salary you want, you'll likely get only what the buyer *wants* to pay—not what he or she is *willing* to pay.

So how do you figure out what you're worth to ensure that you don't price yourself out of the market or sell your services too cheaply? Valuing yourself is a mind game as well as a tactical maneuver.

Step 1. Begin your research. Be confident and assume you are worth whatever the highest-paid person in your position is worth. That's a nice benchmark. To find out how much such a person makes, ask trusted colleagues what they know about salary ranges. Call a headhunter, surf the Internet for industry articles and job sites. Also, call former colleagues as well as the human resources department at previous employers. Leslie Grossman suggests asking "the going rate" for someone in your position and with your experience, and also asking what the highest paid *man* in your position is paid at a particular company. If you have strong relationships with former colleagues—even human resources personnel—they will probably tell you.

Step 2. Establish a personal benchmark based on your research. You may realize that you are currently underpaid, but before you get frustrated and speak to your management in a heated emotional state, stop! Don't say anything . . . yet.

Step 3. Document your accomplishments (pull them from your bragging folder as described in chapter two), and then request a meeting with your boss. This formalizes your request.

Step 4. Ask for a raise. In the meeting, confidently review your accomplishments, emphasizing how you have met and exceeded expectations. Focus on tangible results. End your request by saying that you are worth X amount (whatever number you concluded was your personal benchmark) because you've done research and understand that X is the fair market rate for someone in your position. By requesting a formal meeting, doing your research, and reviewing your accomplishments, your request will not seem arbitrary.

Step 5. If your boss is unwilling to budge, clarify why. Is the denial the result of a budgetary constraint, or is it performance-related? If your boss does not feel your performance is worth more pay, ask for specific areas where you need to improve. Document them and focus on those areas.

Even if you do not get a raise (or if the raise is not the exact amount you asked for), pat yourself on the back. At a minimum, you have made your boss aware that you believe you're worth more money.

When high-tech executive Kim realized she was being paid less than people with the same job in her office, she spoke up:

> *Because I had good connections at work, I discovered that my counterpart was getting a raise and a promotion as an incentive to stay after he threatened to quit. I called up my boss and told him I'd heard about my colleague's raise and then asked when I should be expecting my own raise and promotion. I remember telling him I expected a VP title "in weeks, not months." After he recovered from the shock that I had found out about the promotion, he quickly explained the situation and assured me I was going to be promoted, too. That's how I got my first vice president title.*

◆ **What it takes:** Do your research and you'll probably find out that you're worth more than you think. Then, ask for it.

Don't Work for Free

One of my biggest pet peeves is people who consistently work for free. I constantly see consultants, public speakers, writers, musicians, artists, and designers working for no money. Granted, pay is not the only type of "value" one gets from work; fulfillment, satisfaction, an ego boost, enjoyment, artistic expression, and altruism are all valid forms of compensation. But too often and too easily, people accept such psychic rewards in lieu of being paid for their effort and expertise.

A few things to remember before you give your talent away for free. First, whomever you so generously volunteer your time to is, most likely, making money off you. Second, you will actually increase your perceived worth by attaching a monetary value to your expertise. At the very least, do what I do: set a fee for your services, and if whoever hires you is not able to match it, either politely decline or determine if there is a true upside that justifies your pay cut, such as a charitable cause or a rich networking opportunity. When it comes to work opportunities, it is not easy for me to turn down a hundred bucks here and there, but having educated myself on going rates for consulting and public speeches, I know what I am worth.

◆ **What it takes:** Don't give yourself away for free. You not only lose money you deserve but undervalue your worth in the eyes of others.

Negotiate Compensation Packages You Deserve

Admission: even though I was not about to ask for $12,000 a year after graduation, I was cowardly and clueless when it came to getting what I was worth. In my first job out of graduate school, although my starting salary was more than anyone else in my graduating class, I did not negotiate one iota. When Sabre offered me a job, the recruiter quoted me a salary and benefits package and before she could even finish the offer, I eagerly yelped, "Yes, thank you so much. I'll take it!" I was excited with the offer until my first few weeks on the job, when all the other equally ranked and qualified new hires started talking about how they had negotiated more money and extra vacation time. When it eventually came out that I didn't negotiate anything because I thought Sabre would rescind the offer, my male colleagues were shocked. It was not only embarrassing, but they had all negotiated two weeks' vacation while I had none.

◆ **What it takes:** Never accept the first salary offer you hear. Take time to evaluate it and always ask for more money than you are offered.

Nuances of Negotiation

You were just offered a job that you really want, but your potential new boss calls with the salary and the amount is a lot less than you wanted or expected. Unfortunately, you are too nervous to ask for more money. What to do? First, congratulations. You had a number in mind before you got the offer, which is important—it enabled you to recognize that the offer came in low. More good news: there is a way to ask in a less aggressive manner, and it's an approach that has worked for me.

One time I received an offer that was lower than I wanted. First, I thanked the hiring manager for the offer and told him I would get back to him as soon as possible with an answer. Then, I hung up the phone and did some math, calculating my overall "value," which included my current base salary, bonus, vacation accrued, and the monetary value of my 401(k) matching and healthcare benefits—in essence, the value of what I'd be walking away from. I believed I was worth $12,000 more a year, and so I calculated how much that was for every two-week pay cycle. It turned out I wanted only $500 more with every paycheck, a number that was not as daunting as $12,000. I called my prospective boss and said, "I think we are getting close to an acceptable offer. We are really only off by about $500 per paycheck." The hiring manager realized we weren't talking big bucks and upped the offer.

Although I was a bit wiser about negotiating when I left Sabre to join Commerce One, I still had plenty to learn. Before Commerce One even quoted me a salary offer, I mistakenly told them what my base salary was at Sabre. Huge blunder. Jill Hernstat, a San

Francisco–based human resources recruiter, told me that when she recruits candidates, some of her clients, even against her advice, end up paying a person substantially less than their allocated budget for the job because they find out a candidate's previous salary. "Some clients aren't willing to budge. They believe that it's not right to give a huge bump in salary, even if they know the candidate was previously underpaid."

Avoid telling a future employer your current salary. If you must mention it, discuss it in terms of your total compensation package. Remember, your income is not just your base pay, but the value of your performance bonuses, your accrued vacation, any signing money you received, and your company stock, 401(k), and healthcare packages. This is not stretching the truth: it is a completely honest appraisal of your total compensation. And if your new company doesn't have a 401(k) matching plan or doesn't pay annual bonuses, then it should make up for that discrepancy with its salary.

If a potential employer says raising your salary is absolutely not an option, there are other perks that can be negotiated: a signing bonus, stock options, more vacation time, a flexible schedule, paid mobile phone bills, home office expenses, or an accelerated salary review period—for example, six months instead of a year. Natalie Humphreys, a corporate recruiter for a top computer company, explains how she determines new-hire salaries: "I have to know a person's salary range so I know if I should even consider her for a position. But when you talk about salary, it's okay to speak about acceptable salary ranges and discuss your total overall package needs. But don't overinflate your earnings, because if I find out you've lied, I won't even consider hiring you." Not getting hired is one problem, but inflating or commanding too high a salary is another. Humphreys adds that she may consider you overqualified and not put you through the interview process—also a risk if you are looking for a career change and may be agreeable to certain tradeoffs.

If you dislike your current job, do not tell your prospective employer. As soon as you say, "I can't wait to get out of there," an interviewer smells desperation and will be more likely to lowball you on salary and less inclined to meet your requests.

◆ **What it takes:** Evaluate creative ways to negotiate your salary, and remember, your employment package is not just about the money—be prepared to negotiate everything.

Be Willing to Walk Away from—or Accept—a Lower Salary

You get a job offer for less than you believe you should be paid, and despite asking for more money you are told that the offer is final. First, do not feel guilty for asking; all the men who also got job offers asked, too. Now you must decide: should you stay and work for less, or should you walk away? That depends on two factors:

- Is there a sense of urgency for taking the new job (e.g., you desperately need to leave your present job or require immediate income)?
- Does the new job have nonmonetary benefits that make up for the lack of pay (e.g., career growth opportunities; a chance to get your foot in the door in a new job role or new industry; less stress; shorter hours; more vacation; greater flexibility)?

As Commerce One suffered through the Internet bust, the company began to shrink as management sold off some of its underperforming business units. Feeling that I had tapped my potential at the company, I began interviewing, and I started talking to a well-respected upcoming technology company based in Austin, Texas. The company was looking for someone with my background and skill set to manage large accounts. I went through seven rounds of interviews and was offered the job at a salary that was $50,000 a year less than I currently made. The company knew my current salary range, but they also knew that I was ready to leave Commerce One; the company thought its offer of stock options and the promise of making millions in an initial public offering was enough to lure me. (Um, did they not see that at Commerce One I had already lived the dream *and* the nightmare?) I knew what my minimum acceptable salary level was, and the offer was nowhere near it. I went down my list of strategies: I tried to negotiate more options, a signing bonus, an early performance review, even additional responsibilities commensurate with a higher salary. Nothing worked, and the woman in charge of hiring finally said, "We're just not making progress." She was right—I walked away. I simply would not have felt good taking the job at that salary, and I stayed at Commerce One until the market picked up. About 15 months later I accepted a job offer at another technology company. That job did have a minor pay cut, but the benefits were worth the decrease—namely, greater opportunity for career growth, a chance to build a new company, and less business travel.

You may also elect to take a job for less money when nonmonetary benefits make up for a difference in pay. For example, if you are transitioning to a new industry or a new position, it may be necessary that you make a financial sacrifice as a trade-off for what you lack in experience. For example, many people I know who moved to sales positions had to take a cut in base pay. However, once they figured out the process for closing deals, their overall salary usually grew substantially as sales commissions began to roll in. The reverse is also true. Salespeople who move to another kind of job, such as marketing, can usually count on a cut in pay but find other rewards: less travel, more diversity in day-to-day job assignments, and less stress to make an annual sales quota.

◆ **What it takes:** Know what you are worth, and don't accept less unless there is a truly desirable trade-off (or you really are desperate).

Promote Yourself: Ask for a Raise

Several times, bosses have handed me new responsibilities, a new title, or a new job inside my company—and only a few times have they broached the issue of a salary increase. I could have easily transferred to any number of jobs without a salary bump.

In the case of the aforementioned Commerce One negotiation—which may have you wondering what happened after I mistakenly revealed my present salary—the company's first offer was the same salary for an account manager position, essentially my former pay and title. To counter, I prepared an argument to illustrate why I was worth more. For example, the relationships I had at Sabre with its major clients such as IBM, Merrill Lynch, and JPMorgan Chase would be valuable to Commerce One because I could bring in new business. Thus my "value" was not simply my expertise, but my relationships. I used this and other reasons to justify why I should be hired as a senior account manager with a higher salary, but alas, they did not take my bait and only nudged my base salary and the signing bonus up a tad.

Because I was not willing to walk away from the Commerce One offer (I wanted to work with a potentially lucrative Internet company), I accepted the job knowing I deserved senior status. Within a few months my boss must have agreed because he called me and said, "Congratulations, you've just been promoted to senior account manager." When I asked when I could expect my pay increase, he said it was a promotion in recognition only. I declined the offer, saying I wanted to remain at the more junior level until the salary was commensurate with the new responsibilities. Within two weeks, the new salary came, and so did the title. This time when I asked, I got what I deserved.

From that experience, I maintain a policy: I refuse to accept a long-term increase in job responsibility without more money. Instead, when managers ask me about taking on a new role, I say something like, "Yes, I'm really interested but want to talk about my compensation package. I assume the new job is a director level; how will my pay and options package change?" My language conveys the assumption of a promotion, as well as my confidence that I deserve more money and will get it. I often follow up with, "Would you check with human resources to see what the maximum salary bump is for the job role?" I can't recall a time when I asked and did not receive.

Jeni, an account manager for a major industrial chemicals company, tells her story:

When I was first offered a job and negotiated my salary, my boss told me I was hired at "top dollar" because I had my MBA. I believed him. A few weeks after I started, I found out that a man who began at the same time in the same role, without his MBA, had a much higher salary. I didn't bring it up immediately but decided to wait until I had more facts to prove my worth. I started keeping a list of all my accomplishments, every new deal I closed, every new account I penetrated that others did not. When it was time for my review, I outlined what I had achieved, noting that I had the largest territory and the largest sales growth—never bringing up the fact that I also was the only woman. I told them I expected a 40 percent raise. They agreed! My boss told me I was lucky, because the company historically never gave anything but 4 percent increases. Lucky? I don't think so. I got what I deserved!

◆ **What it takes:** Do not accept more long-term responsibility without more money unless there is a desirable trade-off. If you were turned down for a raise in the past, do not let the experience deter you from asking for more money in the future. Eventually, you will get what you deserve.

Worst-Case Scenarios

Even if you asked for a raise and were denied, you already avoided the worst-case scenario: regret. Nothing is worse than accepting a job or a promotion and later realizing you could have had more money if you had only asked.

No *Is Just a Word—Don't Be Afraid of Hearing It*

It is never easy to take a stand. Even when women know we deserve more, we hesitate to ask for money because we fear hearing the word no. A friend of mine had been working for a company for five years and was promoted year after year without a raise. Eventually, her boss asked her to take on additional job responsibilities, which prevented her from traveling for business, a perk that had allowed her to make up to $30,000 a year more in per diem bonuses. When she accepted the prestigious new job role, she assumed a hefty raise would follow. It didn't. She was actually handling more job responsibilities for less money. We planned different ways she could approach her boss to address the issue of getting more money, and she was all prepped and ready to walk into her office and request her overdue and justifiable increase in salary. But when she arrived at work, she never asked! She was afraid that her manager would say, "No, times are tough and we can't afford it," and that asking would strain their relationship. Argh! I wanted to scream, because she was worth at least double her present income. Worse, she knew it.

What's so frightening about the word no? The actual chances that your supervisor will growl, "No, you don't deserve it," are minute. The chances he or she will say, "No, we don't currently have it in the budget," are much greater.

Simply asking for a raise plants the seed in your manager's mind that you are expecting to be compensated according to the value you've tied to your performance, and if your bosses value you as an employee, they will make an effort to keep you happy so you don't look elsewhere.

◆ **What it takes:** Don't let your fear of rejection dictate your actions, or your income will suffer.

You're Not Worthy

Let's pretend your request has been denied because, your boss says, you have not yet demonstrated performance worthy of more money. Don't be discouraged—you still come out ahead, because if you hadn't asked for the raise you would not have known you and your boss had different perspectives of your expected performance level and worth. This is your opportunity to clarify any misunderstanding your boss may have about your work or any misunderstanding you may have of what's expected of you.

Get a laundry list of areas where you need to demonstrate improvement, and in three to six months come back to your manager and ask to revisit your request. If you agree on a formal review, write the goals down and send them to your boss. If it's more informal, shoot your boss a note saying, "Thanks for your time today reviewing areas where you'd like to see me improve. I understand you would like me to excel in the following ways." Bullet the specific areas, and wind the e-mail up with, "I'll be focusing on these over the next few months so that next time we review my performance you'll be congratulating me on my promotion." Such a casual note is a great way to set your expectations in a nonthreatening fashion and have documented deliverables to revisit with your boss.

◆ **What it takes:** Be persistent and professional. A denied raise is not necessarily a dead end. A future raise is in store if you consistently deliver results and ask for what you are worth.

For Love or Money—or Both?

Despite all my preaching about recognizing your maximum value, money should not be your only goal, a lesson those of us who rode the dot.com boom learned.

At age 28, I was an account director at Commerce One, managing complicated software implementations, making approximately $140,000 per year. The company's stock soared for a period of eight months, and at its height, trading at about $1,000 per share pre-split, my stock was worth over a million dollars. The little girl who saved every penny was suddenly a millionaire—at least on paper. It was exciting, but it was twisted. I started feeling like I deserved such wealth, which was crazy considering I was so young in my career and just happened to be in the right place at the right time, working in a hot industry during a stock market bubble.

In addition to my exaggerated sense of value, there was another problem: I did not feel as happy as I thought I would be, or should be.

After spending my career working toward such a nest egg, I had to go through the dot.com boom *and* bust to change my definition of success. Up to that point I'd always focused on the future. I always wanted to be somewhere else tomorrow instead of enjoying where I was today: as a kid I was so determined to make money that I opted out of trips with friends so I could work, and as an adult I was so intent on getting promotions that I let personal relationships crumble. I was always looking for the next big thing, and when the biggest possible thing found me—millions of dollars in stock, thanks to the market bubble—I was suddenly left without goals and without a future to work for because I thought I had achieved what I was striving for: financial security. But once I had it, I was not even happy in my career. I had spent too much time focusing on attaining the next big thing rather than on enjoying the moment.

When the bubble burst—and my stock's value with it—I was of course disappointed, but I finally realized that the quest for wealth should no longer be my driving motivation for work. That is not to say I abandoned my hunger for money—I just realized it needed to be coupled with a hunger for a more intrinsic type of satisfaction.

Another dot.com survivor, Christy Jones, founded enterprise software firm pcOrder in the late 1990s, and more recently she founded Extend Fertility, a company that allows women to harvest their eggs earlier in life to improve the odds of a later-in-life successful pregnancy. Here's her story:

> By my mid twenties, I was president of a successful technology firm that at the height of the market in 1999 was worth over $2 billion. Before age 30, I was on the cover of Forbes three times. After the market slowed, my company decided to merge back with our parent company, and I managed the integration. I soon realized that selling enterprise software was no longer in my heart, and I felt somewhat lost. I researched many different industries and businesses, from Fortune 500 companies to start-up businesses. I even briefly considered a career in politics.

Through this process, I learned that what I loved most was starting and building things. At that time, I read Sylvia Ann Hewlett's Creating a Life: Professional Women and the Quest for Children, *a book about how a large number of high-performing women were childless. I realized that I was one of those women, and many of my friends were either single, newly married, or having difficulty starting families and going through fertility treatment. I did research and decided to start Extend Fertility in 2002. Certainly I look at everything from a business perspective, so making money is important, but I knew I also needed to build something I could be passionate about for the next decade, something that could change the lives of women. It's very rewarding to get mail from women saying "thank you."*

There is a moral to Christy's and my personal financial stories: resist the urge to flock to a job for only love *or* only money. Work is not just about attaining financial security, nor is it solely about satisfying your soul desires. Great careers are those that deliver both money and personal fulfillment.

◆ **What it takes:** Work for both love *and* money. They need not be mutually exclusive.

I write all this to you as a 30 year old, admittedly young in my career but having learned some lessons that many people do not digest until much later. I still love making money, and I still save lots of it. But these days I try to only accept jobs I will enjoy and feel good about. Writing this book is one such experience.

I believe now more than ever that life is about creating meaningful experiences and fun stories to share with friends, family, and future generations. Over the years I have evolved from a mind-set where I had difficulty taking a week's vacation because I translated it into a week's salary loss to a mind-set that believes a paycheck is worthless if you don't take some time to spend it on experiences. Proof that I changed? I gave up my job—and a six-figure salary—for the once-in-a-lifetime experience of being on a reality television show, a show that brought me back to my roots of selling lemonade on a street corner, only this time in New York City.

No Crying in the Boardroom

Emotions at Work

Our ability to be in touch with feelings—our own and those of others—is a powerful tool in our work. It helps us build relationships, accurately assess situations, and communicate with a variety of people. At the same time, emotions can also harm us in the workplace. While emotional connections serve us well, emotional outburst can derail us (and our careers). And if you want to move up, learning how to channel your emotions into constructive behavior is a must. It's not easy, especially when it's not in your nature to hide feelings: a rosy blush, watery eyes, a raised voice, clenched jaw, or the worst, crying. Eruptions of sadness, anger, and jealousy overshadow objective thought, diminish productivity, and, like it or not, tarnish one's credibility.

While I am a strong advocate of silencing unproductive emotional outbursts, I am not suggesting that we check all emotion at the office door. Both women and men thrive professionally when, for example, they combine intelligence and intuition to read people or mix knowledge and empathy to build relationships. Head and heart is a powerful combination. Unfortunately, I think most men lean toward using the former while women often rely on the latter. Having worked side by side with men, I realize that while they still feel strongly about matters, they are less likely to confuse *having* emotion with *reacting* based on emotion. But at the same time, men can be out of touch with feelings—especially the feelings of others—and hence they miss valuable opportunities to build relationships and motivate others.

I never let anyone see me cry at the office. I won't say that I have never cried at work, but I will say that, publicly, I only show emotions that I believe my colleagues are comfortable dealing with. Is this fake? No way! It's smart. I believe I read people and tap aspects of my personality accordingly to make others feel comfortable. It's just common sense: if presented with a serious business situation, I speak firmly, loudly, and with a steady voice. If a team needs a cheerleader, I serve up a pep talk in a friendly, spirited tone.

Some of you may be frustrated and may feel that I'm telling you to pretend to be someone you are not. But I am not saying don't be true to yourself—just that coworkers do not have to see every facet of your personality or every feeling you experience. Emotions can blind us in business, and they can also light the way. It's all about awareness and the ability to tune into yourself as well as others.

Be Mistress of Your Emotional Domain

Be in control of your emotions at all times, and at the very least be aware of how they are affecting your behavior in the workplace. If you allow your feelings to control you, emotional outbursts such as yelling and crying will only make others uncomfortable and curtail rather than further your cause.

Don't Confuse Passion with Emotion

One of the biggest errors I believe women make at work is confusing passion with emotion. For example, I've seen more than one woman operate under the mistaken belief that allowing herself to tear up in front of the boss is okay because the boss will truly understand her level of conviction for the project. Or she may think raising her voice and getting upset when people don't agree with her decision merely shows her colleagues how passionate she is about her job. And should an unfortunate turn of events trigger her to sling curse words and insults, she simply assumes others will be impressed by her dedication to perfection.

Ah, no.

Consider the three primary definitions for the word passion: 1) an intense, overpowering emotion, or expression of emotion, such as love, joy, hatred, or anger; 2) a subject that is the object of somebody's intense interest or enthusiasm; and of course, 3) a strong sexual desire (but we'll leave that for another book).

In workplace settings, women tend to confuse definition one, the act of expression, with the definition two, a state of enthusiasm. You can be enthusiastic without crying, yelling, or using angry language. Such behavior only renders other colleagues, especially men, speechless, and not because they are impressed with your undying devotion, but because they don't know what the hell to do with the red-faced, misty-eyed, fire-spitting woman who has invaded their comfort zone. In short, emotional outbursts stump men on the home front, and it's no different at the office. Frankly, most men are not quite sure how to respond when a woman turns on the temper tantrums. Any outpouring of tears or four-letter words only distracts everyone from business matters. Suddenly, the only thing your colleagues care about is shutting you up so they don't feel so awkward. Marketing manager Lynne shares her past experience:

> *I received an annual review from a boss who historically only promoted men. I had worked very hard the previous year and completed many significant accomplishments recognized by the*

CEO, and I had received company awards and rewards. Not only did I get a mediocre review, but I was due for a promotion and didn't get it. I cried in his office. It was the only time I have cried at work in my career. My boss had a stay-at-home wife, and I think the look on his face when I started bawling was not that of a sympathetic manager but of a husband or father who hated to see his little "girl" cry. My boss did not know what to do! The whole situation was horrible, and he ended up taking back the review, giving me the minimum number of points to escalate me to the next performance level. It was a slap in the face. Three years later I still work for the same boss and we are still feeling the pains of the conflict.

Now, I am not a passion smasher. Personally, I am passionate about achieving results in whatever I do. But I do believe women can be too emotional in the workplace and use passion as an excuse for an inability to control outbursts.

◆ **What it takes:** Express passion by hard work, dedication, and in-novative ideas—not tears and unnecessary drama.

Control the Nasty Emotions

Yes, you will have days when you feel like a little girl inside and want to simply curl up in your daddy's arms and cry, complain to your mom over chicken-noodle soup, and hurl your (appropriately high) heels at your boss. I have those days when emoting is all I want to do. But we can't give in. You rarely hear men indulging in a loud poor-me whine, and while they may yell, male anger is more acceptable than a female's. When a man raises his voice he is not cast as a drama king or criticized for being too emotional. He may be called insane or even a jerk, but more often than not he is revered for doing his job rather than reprimanded for letting his feelings get in the way of his job.

It's not fair, but until women have more influence over the workplace and boxes of tissues are passed out as readily as free golf balls, I strongly suggest you put on your game face and keep intense expressions of frustration, anger, fear, disappointment, and antagonism out of the office if you want to be heard. It's not easy, but emotional control will definitely help you move up—and once you do, you can change the rules.

◆ **What it takes:** Control over-the-top emotional expression at the office. It will impede your professional ascent.

Don't Catch the Negative Energy

For a while as I worked my way up at Sabre, I managed the software implementation of web-based travel systems for large corporations. It was exactly where I wanted to be: working in the company's hottest division, e-commerce, and with top customers— Merrill Lynch, IBM, McKinsey & Company, and JPMorgan Chase. It was a great opportunity and ultimately led to my career in e-commerce. However, I began with a very bad start.

There were a few women in my department—in similar roles but in other regions—and I was warned about their "bad attitudes." Apparently, they were not happy because they felt that the product did not work as well as customers expected and that the company wasn't doing enough about it. These women worked too many hours and felt no one appreciated them. Initially, I was not worried about catching the negative bug—because I was so elated about the new opportunity—but after about three months I found myself itching with their illness. My traditional optimism had dissipated, and my newfound frustration channeled into unproductive outlets. I looked for problems rather than solutions and bitched about hiccups rather than solving them quickly. Eventually, I simply burned out and began looking for other positions at the company.

The women's negativity was contagious. How had I caught it? First, I spent too much time with them, participating in conversations that bred pessimism. I also stopped prioritizing and separating problems I could control from those I could not. Instead of focusing on circumstances I could change, I focused on everything and became overloaded and unproductive. A vicious circle. I should have directed my limited energy into problems I at least had a chance of solving. I should have set boundaries on my time and not let work become a 24/7 obsession; I had no other outlet for all the negative energy I was accruing.

◆ **What it takes:** Run, don't walk, away from watercooler whiners. If you're surrounded, maintain perspective and prioritize your time.

Pick Your Bitching—and Your Battles

When I first began working with customers, I was so focused on making them deliriously happy and successful that I lobbied hard for every single change to my company's software that the client wanted. If the customer mentioned an off-the-cuff wish that the software application had a blue background rather than a gray background, or that it displayed the user's name in Arial font rather than Times, I'd argue it to the product managers with the same gusto that I argued for critical functionality, like fixing the bug that displayed incorrect airline fares. I never told the customer no. Instead, I pushed my company, claiming I was "the voice of the customer!" The result? Many of my requests were not met. I had drowned myself out as the girl who cried, "Customer service!" too many times.

Not all battles are worth fighting, and not all problems are worth complaining about. Fight or whine about every little thing and you lose credibility and waste your own energy.

My managers recognized my focus on customer satisfaction, but they didn't think I could manage expectations. They were right; my need to please got in the way. Now I continue to hear out every request so customers know I am aware of their needs, but then I ask them to prioritize their requests so I know which are critical. For those issues, I go to bat.

As for whining, anecdotes such as this speak for themselves:

At a recent meeting with the boss of my company and a colleague—both women—I sat and listened as the manager whined and carried on about how another woman in the office had stolen her idea and that it just wasn't fair she didn't get credit. After fifteen minutes, I think the boss couldn't have cared less. . . . She was staring out the window as if to scream, "Stop whining!" My colleague had no clue. I was personally embarrassed for her, carrying on the way she did. Her fifteen minutes in front of the boss could have been spent doing something more productive, like showing her competence.

Instead of communicating with facts—for example, explaining how she came up with the original idea—the whiny woman focused only on feelings of frustration and anger.

◆ **What it takes:** Manage your emotions. Don't let your feelings dictate the message you deliver or how to deliver it.

Think Before You Act and React

I was in a company-wide meeting when my boss, while speaking about my account, told everyone, "We don't know the issues of our customer well enough. . . ." I have no idea what he said after that because my body temperature immediately elevated, my face went red, my hands started shaking. I was the account manager, and I was outraged that he had the nerve to say—in front of the entire company—that I was doing a lousy job. I felt he might as well have announced, "Amy sucks," through a megaphone.

After the meeting I stomped into his office. "John," I said. "Because I am the only woman in this office you are going to have to deal with my emotions right now, because I am sooooo mad!" I hurled questions at him: Do you think I am doing a bad job? Do you think I don't have a strong relationship with the client? Am I misrepresenting the account to the company? While I was ranting and raving, John began to chuckle. Then he smiled and essentially said, "Calm down and breathe. I was simply stating that as a company we all need to think more about our customers' needs, not our own requirements. It had absolutely nothing to do with your performance." Sigh. Relief. All the negative emotions whipped into frenzy out of my erroneous assumption suddenly disappeared. Now, I was simply embarrassed at my outburst.

I should have politely asked John to review his public comments with me, alone, so I could mine him for more information. And if I still was not certain what he meant, I could have asked if there was anything I could do to improve my relationship with the client. The result would have been the same, save my ranting.

◆ **What it takes:** Because emotions can trump reality, make sure your response is justified before you act (or react).

Communicate Your Message with Tolerance

I am hard on myself, always have been. And I am hard on others, and I confess I have very little patience with underperformers. In fact, in one job review, I was told I should be more tolerant of people who did not always perform at levels that I expected of myself. So, like the emotionally savvy professional I want to be, I have learned a more acceptable way to communicate my disappointment when expectations are not met—and still get the results I desire. For years I have indulged in what Hellen Davis, a career coach and president of Indaba, Inc., calls giving subordinates emotional "wiggle room." She is not implying we let people off the hook by pretending we are satisfied with shoddy work. Rather, Davis says emotional wiggle room can be granted in the way we express disappointment. Rather than leveling folks with the full force of our anger—"You are doing a terrible job! Why can't you complete anything on time?"—we can get the same point across with a bit of drama, wit, and a raised eyebrow: "I'm going to kiiillll yoooouuuu and pull all my hair out if you don't get this assignment completed on time." I've actually walked into a room of developers and said just that, in my best singsong, semi-serious voice. Of course, no one believes I am actually going to harm them. I actually think they'd prefer to hear mock threats of death than hear "Your work is late! You'd better get it done now!"

Emotional wiggle room means you express the seriousness of the situation with a dose of humor. Call it passive-aggressive, but it works. Lack of emotional wiggle room could be seen on *The Apprentice*, when contestant Omarosa bluntly told her teammate Jessie, "You were terrible" at negotiation and when, in front of Donald Trump, she said that her teammate Heidi "wasn't always professional, didn't have much class or finesse."

◆ **What it takes:** If you're prone to intolerance, make a conscious effort to soften the way you express it. You'll get the results you expect faster and more effectively than if you are overly harsh.

Manage Your Personal Life at Work

Truly tragic life events are important for you to address at work so others know you are under a unique stress. Sit down with the people you work closely with every day and calmly explain the situation to them. Tell them what, if anything, you need from them, to serve as a backup contact for your clients, or to make sure they track you down if a family member calls, and what they can expect from you, such as leaving early or appearing distracted. They'll appreciate your honesty and give you more wiggle room.

That said, try not to use coworkers as your daily sounding board. As much as they care about your plight (though some will not care), they still have work to get done. When Alexis, now a pharmaceutical sales rep, found out her father was diagnosed with late-stage pancreatic cancer, she was finishing her graduate thesis and working a demanding internship at a hospital. When her father finally passed away after a yearlong struggle to stay alive to see his daughter graduate, Alexis had to mourn his death *and* begin a new job. At both the internship and her first job, Alexis learned a lot about how coworkers handle someone else's personal tragedy.

> When I told people at work about my father's illness, some were very understanding, others were just worried I would not be able to focus on my job, and still others assumed I wouldn't be able to handle it and did not give me assignments I wanted. They essentially demoted me when what I needed most was to be involved in work to keep my mind busy. Maybe it would have been different if I were a man. Maybe they would have assumed I could handle the pressure instead of assuming I would let work slide. The reality is that most of your colleagues want to see you functioning at 100 percent because anything less means more work

for them. Express too much sadness or grief in front of people who can make or break your professional life, and you'll be misconstrued as too emotional and not capable of operating under high pressure.

Even without expressing much sadness in front of others, Alexis was cast as the grief-stricken daughter and incompetent worker. When bad days hit and you need some space, negotiate it rationally and not in an emotional or volatile manner. For example, if someone hands you a last-minute assignment with an immediate deadline, rather than explode about why they don't recognize your fragile state, calmly say that next time you need more notice and will do your best to get the project back to them as soon as possible. Don't weave in the personal at every turn. Also, find one person you can confide in and keep your talk of personal issues relegated to him or her, as well as friends and family. How you handle personal stress will communicate how you handle professional stress. Fair or not, that's how it goes.

◆ **What it takes:** Serious personal problems that may distract you from work or interrupt your workflow should be addressed discretely and professionally.

Safe Havens: When the Dam Breaks

You can't hold it in. You are fuming. You are pissed. You want to scream bloody murder and the tears are coming and you can't stop them. All right. Let it out . . . strategically.

Keep Your Eyes Wide Open
You feel the tears well up, but excusing yourself from the meeting is not an option. When this happens to me, I open my eyes as

wide as possible so air comes into my eyes—and dries them out—and keeps me from crying. A friend of mine pinches herself in between her index finger and thumb, creating a painful distraction to block her from bursting into tears. A third strategy comes from Hellen Davis, the executive coach who was, in a former career incarnation, a parachuting instructor for the military. Davis advises female executives to ward off inappropriate blushing or tears by looking straight ahead and above the invisible horizon line, up to the ceiling. To others you will appear to be in deep thought. Davis says this has a physiological effect that kicks the brain into visual rather than emotional mode. Feel free to try any of them. I'm sticking to my eyes-wide-open trick.

When All Else Fails, Yell

That's what men do all too often, right? Yelling is more acceptable at work, definitely better than tears. My former colleague Kim advises, "If you feel like you are going to cry, scream something like, 'This is outrageous!' If, after you scream, you still feel like you may cry, leave the room. It's better to let others think they pushed you too far than that they broke you."

Call on Your "Bench" Buddy

Hopefully, there is at least one person in your company who you trust implicitly, a true confidant. Maybe it is your mentor, your assistant, or the woman down the hall. This is the person to whom you can dump anything. Complain. Bitch. Cry. Whatever. The problem is, unless you both have an office, you have to find a private place to hash it out.

A journalist I once met had such a trusted friend. Around the corner from her office building was a simple stone bench secluded in the shadowy entrance of another building. It was virtually invisible to passersby, and whenever the journalist or her cohort had an immediate need to get something off her chest, all one had to say to the other was, "Bench!" and before anyone knew it they had left the building together in silence, escaped to their secret bench, and were talking and emoting up a storm. Inevitably, within ten minutes, the upset person had calmed down, felt relieved, and was ready to return to work.

Find Salvation in the Restroom

Cubicle culture does not offer anyone much privacy. So, if you do not have an office door to shut, escape to the bathroom! This is your Switzerland, your neutral territory: just like the old slogan for Las Vegas, what happens here, stays here. (I think this is some unwritten but understood rule among women in business.)

No man is going to see you sob—in the restroom. No one is going to come after you—in the restroom. You can sit in a stall for an hour and no one will bother you. In the restroom, tissues are plentiful and privacy is guaranteed.

Keep Quiet

So you couldn't make it to the restroom in time and someone sees you crying in the hallway. Guess what? No one has to know what you are upset about. If people ask, you don't owe them an answer or an honest explanation. For all they know, something tragic happened in your personal life, which is none of their business. Resist the need to air your grievance to anyone who intercepts you in the hall. When they ask, "What's wrong? Are you okay?" just say, "I'm fine, thanks," and keep moving.

Get Physical

Not only does exercise keep you fit and looking your best, it is a critical outlet for stress. When I am frustrated and frazzled at work, I get out of the office, go put on my running shoes, and hit the road or take a heated yoga class where I sweat off enough steam to refocus and think clearly. Getting your heart rate up regularly through exercise is a great way to improve your productivity and improve your mental health.

Attention! You are Not the Center of All Criticism

One of the reasons I believe women upset so easily is because we feel personally attacked when someone disagrees with or criticizes us. Men, on the other hand don't.

While at Thanksgiving dinner with a group of people, two of my male friends were recounting the knock-down, drag-out fight they had the night before (it was over a woman). They had literally gotten to the point where they were not only yelling but fist-fighting! Yet, here they were, less than 24 hours later, laughing and asking the other to please pass the wine. I was shocked that, after such a dispute, they were not only civil to each other but back to being best of friends. One of them explained it to me: "I wasn't mad at *him*, I was just mad at what he *did*."

While not a business-related anecdote, this scenario plays itself out in the workplace all the time. Try adopting the same mind-set next time you find your eyes welling up with tears when your boss tells you to modify the contents of your presentation or disagrees with your opinion on how to handle a customer. If your overall performance is a problem, you can be sure your boss will tell you in a more formal situation. So in the moment, realize that your boss is commenting on a specific issue.

Katie, a public relations manager, did just that:

I recently started a new job and had my first assignment: prepare a marketing and sales presentation for our field sales team about a customized, on-line news service we wanted to sell to our clients. I spent days thoroughly preparing my presentation to impress my new boss and presented him with my materials. After I finished delivering the presentation, he said, "This is going to need a lot of work. It will probably go through thirty revisions." A while back in my career, I would have taken that comment personally and been upset with his critique of my work, but I know that overall he was satisfied with the draft version and he only requested changes where he thought we could improve the overall content and create a win-win for the entire company. I knew he was not directly attacking me—he just wanted the presentation to be perfect!

I learned not to take disagreements personally during the debate classes I took years ago, which for whatever reason were mostly populated by young men. In debate class, you argue both for and against a specific subject. I remember that a young woman in the class once got incredibly upset when someone rebutted her argument about prison expansion in the United States. Hello? If there's no disagreement, there's no debate. Having watched the others in the class, I knew that people can fight a point without fighting each other.

◆ **What it takes:** Don't take things personally. Recognize the difference between being personally attacked and professionally critiqued.

Business As Usual: Your Idea Sucks

Disagreement can be effective and productive—provided people disagree in appropriate ways. At work, we often have brainstorming sessions with the understanding that no ideas are stupid. The only rule is to keep the creative juices flowing because ideas, even bad ones, spark more ideas. When we finish the brainstorming, it's time to play devil's advocate, and we challenge each and every idea until we reach the best solution. As a result, we accomplish the ultimate goal: to find the best overall decision.

It's refreshing to work in an environment where criticism is viewed as a means of development rather than mistreatment. If you adopt this perspective you'll find it easier to take criticism less personally and less emotionally. When we assume criticism is personal and not professional we risk inflicting harm on ourselves worse than hurt feelings. Private investor and author Kathy Elliott invests money in early-stage companies and routinely interviews entrepreneurs about their business plans. As part of her role, Elliott evaluates financial forecasts, marketing models, and product designs to test the company's long-term potential as well as its founders' business acumen. It is Elliott's job to look for problems. She has seen female entrepreneurs, when faced with questions that challenge their ideas, get riled and defensive. Their tone changes, their voices rise in objection rather than discussion, and sometimes they completely shut down, unable to address valid concerns. As a result, says Elliott, these women are less likely to convince an investor to ante up thousands of dollars to start their companies, although their ideas and their business skill may be as solid as or superior to their male counterparts'. Part of selling oneself and being effective in business is the ability to remove oneself emotionally from a situation, or, as Elliott says, "roll with the punches." Indeed, business requires sifting through and rejecting ideas so the best ones surface.

◆ **What it takes:** Understand that rejection, disagreements, and criticism are all expected in the course of business. Don't worry when someone disagrees with you; worry if no one ever does.

Caution: Assumptions Ahead

Two sources of misplaced emotion are: 1) erroneous assumptions that others make about you and your behavior, and 2) erroneous assumptions you make about others. The first is difficult to control, the second a bit easier. I was working with an important client about to take its software "live," and my customer wanted me onsite in the event problems arose. Before the launch, my company's regional director—a woman—called and asked me to fly to San Francisco immediately to help close a deal. I told her, "No, I'm sorry, I can't go," because I had a previous client obligation. She, however, heard something like, "Nope. I don't want to help *you*! *You* and *your* initiatives are not important to me." She interpreted my no as a value judgment on an activity that was important to her; she also assumed that I purposely wanted to impede her work progress and make her look bad. After yelling at me over the phone for 15 minutes, she also did not speak to me for two weeks. She misinterpreted my rejection of a situation as a rejection of her and my behavior as a personal insult. There was not much I could do but let her calm down.

You can, however, prevent yourself from making emotionally charged assumptions about others. Executive coach Helen Davis suggests "reframing the context of your perception" to prevent personalizing issues to a degree that they usher in an unproductive emotional response. Objectively check your emotional response and ask yourself if your negative feelings are really warranted given the situation. Consulting director Lori recalls how she handled one such situation:

> *While working with a woman who was notorious for degrading team members in public by yelling and screaming, I grew tired of basically being verbally abused every Wednesday at 1*

p.m. While my natural tendency was to assume her behavior was based on something I did wrong, I came to understand that it was healthier for me and the team of I took the offensive and refused to engage her (as well as myself) at an emotional level. I started bringing her back to the topic at hand instead of staying in her emotional "swirl." I also took to advising her of controversial issues in private to avoid the public display.

Lori not only viewed the situation objectively and concluded the woman's behavior was a character flaw, she tailored her interaction with the volatile person to minimize the exhausting, offensive behavior.

Sometimes a no, a crazy colleague, or even a wave of silence (such as an unreturned phone call or e-mail) is just that and has nothing to do with you. Don't take these actions personally if they are not obvious attacks against you or if they are related to a person's psyche, not your performance.

◆ **What it takes:** Don't always assume someone else's behavior is about you. Business can get personal, but in most cases it isn't.

Bitch Is Not a Four-Letter Word

My philosophy regarding conflict has changed over the years. In the past I avoided it to prevent having uncomfortable, face-to-face disagreements with people, but I now realize avoiding problems only creates barriers with superiors and people who work for me. Many women avoid confrontation for fear of being labeled a "bitch" or tough. Somehow we've been convinced that dealing with problems head-on is unfeminine. Get over it. Take the *b*-word as a compliment. It means you are a woman who knows what she wants. If you insist on accommodating others' opinions all the time and being sugar and spice and everything nice, then you might as well relegate yourself to a career of serving coffee and answering phones.

As a supervisor, if you never say anything negative to your subordinates, never criticize or disagree, then you are, essentially, not doing your job. Challenge, critique, and guide people who work for you because it helps them improve. Plus, employees think that if their boss never critiques their performance, she is either too scared or incompetent.

I also find it fascinating that while we tend to avoid conflict in the workplace, women feel the need to communicate constantly in personal relationships, even when that means fighting with our significant others. We justify relationship spats by insisting, "Fighting is healthy, it means we are being honest with each other and growing as a couple." So why haven't we figured out how to apply the same philosophy to work relationships? Granted, we can't fight with our boss in the same emotionally fraught vein we argue with our mate. (And we can't make up the same way either, see chapter four about sex in the workplace.) A good professional argument can actually be a good thing to help you move up because you establish a reputation for conviction and self-confidence. Just don't let your emotions invade the professional debate.

◆ **What it takes:** Don't fear being called a bitch. It's just a five-letter word for strong.

Emotional Savvy: Good Emotions at Work

As I said at the beginning of this chapter, there is a definite place for one's more intuitive and more emotional side in the workplace. Emotional connections and feelings can absolutely assist us professionally. People thrive at work when they use intuition to build relationships with clients and colleagues, appreciation and empathy to motivate others, listening skills to resolve conflict, and humility to solve problems and recognize alternative solutions.

As an account director in the technology sector, I usually managed teams of developers who built and customized software to meet my clients' needs. These techies, all men, never met with the client but rather spent their workdays staring at computer screens churning out code and solving complicated technical problems based on our customer requirements. The developers spoke a half-dozen computer languages that were foreign to me, and I was in awe of their ability to create complex programs that automated services. Yet when I voiced my admiration and complimented their technical abilities, the developers fired back, "Are you kidding? Our job is simple compared to yours. You actually have to work with people and deal with their constant demands!"

Of course, this is a matter of perspective, but the techies had a point. I worked with different personalities every day—shy technical consultants, outgoing chief executives, cocky salespeople, chatty administrative assistants—and with all these people, I studied their mood and personality and adjusted my style to work well with them. While the software developers who worked for me could read code, many of the developers could not read people. And while they could rewrite a computer program to meet different business requirements for each client, they were hard-pressed to rewire their own personality to collaborate with different types of individuals. (Those who could do both were priceless.) There is no doubt about it: the ability to communicate effectively—so people deliver high-quality business results on time and on budget despite differences in opinion, style, personality, and mood—is as valuable a talent as technical expertise, finance, or marketing.

"A few years ago, all we really cared about was programming skills; we were not concerned with customer presentability. Now we outsource technical skills overseas and look for people who have the all-in-one package," says Danielle Royston, human resources director for an Austin-based technology company. Muriel Anderson, a business professor at the University at Buffalo, agrees: "You can have the greatest technical skills, but if you do not have people, or so-called soft, skills, then you will have a hard time setting yourself apart from the rest."

♦ **What it takes:** Merge interpersonal skills and awareness with intellect for a winning combination.

Be Emotionally Savvy

In her business courses, professor Anderson teaches a concept known as emotional intelligence, which was formally defined in 1990 by two professors, John Mayer and Peter Salovey. To paraphrase their definition, emotional intelligence is a person's ability to observe and identify one's own and others' feelings and emotions, to discriminate among them, and to use this information to guide one's thinking and action.

Anderson sees emotional intelligence as how effectively people manage their own emotions as well as the emotions of others. She adds that people with high emotional intelligence are, first and foremost, very self-aware. They know their own strengths and weaknesses, and they can stand back and recognize how their behavior affects their own and others' performance. She says that people who are high on the emotional intelligence scale are, for instance, aware not only of what triggers their emotions, but also of the implications of their reactions.

On the other hand, people with low emotional intelligence have little self-awareness, are blind to how their speech and behaviors affect others, and thus they possess no power to alter behavior to achieve a desired outcome. As a result, miscommunication flourishes, disagreements go unresolved, tempers flare, and business outcomes suffer. (Not surprising, people with low emotional intelligence make for good reality television but lousy business.)

I once asked a psychologist if people could control or alter their emotional state. She told me that it is not possible to control one's emotional state but that you can learn to recognize various emotions and understand what causes them. Using her advice, I have made an effort to consciously assess my emotions and have thus become more emotionally savvy. Being emotionally savvy (my own take on emotional intelligence) in business is not so much about changing who you are or avoiding your feelings but rather about understanding your feelings and modifying the way you respond. Some people do this naturally, but for those who do not, Anderson suggests asking people how well they believe you read other people's moods and nonverbal cues. Anderson says that asking your colleagues the following questions (based on a questionnaire put together by the HayGroup) can help you gauge your level of self-awareness, if people are willing to give real answers.

- Do I present myself in an assured and unhesitating manner?
- Do I have a sense of humor about myself?
- Do I have presence? For example, do I stand out in a group?
- Am I aware of my own strengths and weaknesses?
- Am I aware of which emotions I am feeling and why?
- Do I recognize the links between my feelings and what I think, do, and say?
- Am I open to new information about myself?
- Do I recognize how my feelings affect my performance?

Use others' feedback to identify patterns. One person's criticism does not really count; you want to identify recurring themes that you can focus on changing.

While feedback from others is enlightening, it won't serve you unless you want to change your behavior. I like this story from veterinarian Tracy:

A few years ago, I worked as a veterinarian in a large clinic and, after a while, noticed none of the women in the office spoke to me often. I didn't really think about it much, they just kept their distance. One day, I asked a woman in the office what the problem was, and she said all the assistants were afraid of me because they thought I was always mad. I was dumbfounded! I wasn't mad, and I had no clue I gave off that impression. I confronted them with the misunderstanding, and asked them what I did that gave them that idea. They said I never engaged in office chitchat and rarely, if ever, smiled while I worked. I apologized, clarifying that I was just very focused at work. I began making an effort to be friendlier in the office and even gave them free rein to tell me when they thought I was acting harshly. Until I asked about how I acted, I had no idea I was doing anything wrong.

◆ **What it takes:** Mine others for insight into how emotionally savvy you really are. Don't be insulted by their feedback; instead, be empowered to become more emotionally savvy.

Translate Feelings into Productivity

For a specific example of how emotional awareness makes for good business, particularly sales, I'll turn to estate lawyer Elizabeth, who believes that people will be much more likely to bond with you if your goal is to serve customers before servicing your own ego. Elizabeth's millionaire clients have told her that they prefer working with women professionals because "women are not in it for their own ego and there is less conflict of interest." Or at least, women don't come off as self-interested and egotistical. This is where the stereotype of women as nurturers and caretakers works to our advantage. And based on my own experience in sales organizations, I agree that a woman can have an easier time than a man putting a customer ahead of her own interests. I've watched many men sell, and I've often seen their egos start to seep into everything they say. Men are frequently so focused on talking about themselves and their product—for the sheer satisfaction of hearing themselves talk and sound intelligent—that clients lose interest and trust. It's painful to watch. While the customer may be showing obvious signs of skepticism or lack of interest, many men just don't notice—or they don't care. As for women, how many times have you heard females characterized as "slick" or as "used-car" salespeople? As long as we use less ego and more intuition in our pitch and complement it with confidence, professionalism, and knowledge, the negotiation centers on fulfilling a customer need rather than fulfilling our own.

Emotionally savvy women also make great salespeople because they are aware of and adjust to customers' proclivities, moods, and preferences. Being able to read people, a skill the techies in my office admitted they did *not* have, is a talent many women definitely possess. Sales manager Diane read her customer, boosted her sales, and found a new hobby all at the same time:

> *About a decade ago, I sold laundry detergent to retailers, and the store manager at my largest account was a complete bear. I couldn't sell him a case of product to save my life. I tried a wilting-flower demeanor, used all my brand knowledge, and even came to the store during overnight shifts to show him how*

dedicated I was. Nothing worked. Then one day I noticed a NASCAR trinket on his desk. I had never seen a NASCAR event in my life, but I decided I had better start watching. The next time I called on the store manager, I started asking him about the race from the previous weekend. "Could you believe that spin out," etc., etc. But more important than spewing facts, I always asked his opinion and listened more than I talked. It was as if a light went on in his brain, and I proceeded to make this a key discussion topic on all subsequent sales calls. Before I knew it, I was selling him trucks upon trucks of laundry detergent!

◆ **What it takes:** Pay more attention to others than to yourself.

Lead with Your Heart

The most successful leaders I've worked with know how to motivate others by tapping into their emotional core and their need to feel inspired, appreciated, respected, and empowered. Many men in leadership positions do this by acting like a coach, using emotionally raw energy right before a big game. With words and body language, a good coach challenges people to believe in themselves and perform their best—even if they are only selling laundry detergent.

One of the most memorable examples I've seen of leaders who use emotion to motivate was at Mary Kay, the direct-sales cosmetics company where I worked as a product-marketing intern during college. I attended Mary Kay's annual sales conference in Dallas, where thousands of independent sales representatives gather each year to learn about new products and new sales strategies. For a week I listened as company leaders and successful saleswomen delivered emotionally charged speeches. One woman recounted how Mary Kay helped her go from living in a small apartment, working multiple jobs, and being unable to pay

her bills to living in a beautiful home with a stay-at-home husband and, of course, the fabulous pink Cadillac. Rags-to-riches
tales such as that touched everyone at such an emotional level
that even I was wondering why I bothered with college when all
I had to do was sell cosmetics in my neighborhood.

Rallying employees not only to meet sales quotas but to conquer
their own worlds is one reason many organizations hold annual
sales meetings in January, a time of year when everyone is taking
personal stock of the past and strengthening themselves for the future.

In addition to delivering the heartfelt pep talk, crafting
emotionally-aware company policies is another way to motivate
workers. As a partner at her own, predominately female law firm,
Elizabeth points out that one of women's strengths as leaders is to see
colleagues and employees through a more personal lens, as "whole"
human beings. Specifically, she and her legal partners believe that
people feel better when they have control over their lives. As a result,
their firm has a unique compensation system in place for paralegals.
While other law firms pay paralegals a base salary, Elizabeth's firm
has an incentive program whereby paralegals can make unlimited
income if they meet and exceed certain billable-hour goals. Such a
merit-based pay policy has paid off. When the firm recognized the
human need to be in control of one's own destiny, says Elizabeth, her
paralegals became more productive, and the firm profited, too.

◆ **What it takes:** Address others in an emotional light, and you will
motivate them to perform.

Humor: Feel Free to Indulge

After all this talk of using and controlling feelings at work, I
must say that my favorite emotional tool is humor. In fact, when
one is interacting with men, humor bridges the gender divide

nicely. Laughing with colleagues creates a connection that is tough to duplicate, and often the best laughs are found in groups, during meetings, and even out after work. So let your wit loose and your one-liners fly. (Just don't make too much fun of colleagues or superiors—good jokes have a way of circulating.) If you're not a naturally funny person, make it a point to hang around with people who are, and join in the shared laughter. Humor diffuses, it personalizes, it engenders community.

At the very least, humor prevents you from taking yourself too seriously and helps spark new energy. A little humility goes a long way. There I was, having a heated debate with half a dozen colleagues last summer because we couldn't agree about how to develop a solution for my customer. To convey my point, I decided I needed to visualize my idea on the whiteboard. As I confidently jumped up from my desk, my high heel got caught in my briefcase handle. I stumbled slightly, and, as if in slow motion, a colleague lifted his foot to try to stop my forward fall, but his action only increased my speed. Another man who could have easily broken my fall decided instead to jump out of the way. I swiftly face-planted into the wall, only to bounce off and fall gracelessly to the ground. All the men in the room stood still and stared silently in fear and disbelief. Although my head and my knees (and my ego) hurt like hell, I began laughing hysterically, and suddenly, everyone joined in. After marking a bull's-eye on the wall to remember this momentous occasion, we regrouped and then quickly came to agreement on the solution for our customer problem.

◆ **What it takes:** When in doubt, laugh! A sense of humor not only lightens the mood, it increases productivity.

Make Yourself Known

The Importance of Being Recognized

About eight years into my career, I was managing a software implementation project for one of my company's largest customers. I spent my days working at the client's offices with a supporting team of about 20 people. At one point, we ran into serious problems with the new software. Essentially, too many user profiles overloaded the system and caused the software to freeze.

The malfunction was so severe that if it wasn't fixed immediately my company risked losing not only my client but others as well. Determined to prevent the crisis, I created a 30-day plan, and my entire on-site staff and a development team back at headquarters hunkered down to resolve the issue. We held heated meetings with the irate client, and at the onset my team met every four hours to discuss progress. Midnight phone calls were commonplace; everyone was committed to solving the problem and making the customer happy.

As we toiled away, I kept the regional vice president, who spent most of his time back at my company's headquarters, informed about our progress. What I didn't realize, however, was that he was keeping the company's senior executives posted as well, but in a manner that excluded my team and me from the conversation. When my staff and I finally solved the problem and picked our heads up long enough to attend our own company-wide meeting, we sat gaping in disbelief as a senior executive took the stage and thanked the vice president for saving the account. My team's collective thought: "He's got to be kidding." We came up with the plan, we did the work, and someone else took the credit, all of it. My customer didn't even know the VP's name! Sure, I was proud we had solved the problem, and I had received accolades from the customer, but pride and a pat on the back from a client wasn't going to get me promoted. Without recognition or acknowledgment, my efforts were completely invisible, and my chances of moving up—for what I considered one of my biggest professional achievements—looked dim.

I blame myself for what happened. True, it was disappointing that the vice president did not credit us, but I should have never assumed that he would. I should have kept senior executives in the loop on my own (without alienating the VP), either through face-to-face communication or the occasional e-mail status update.

What I learned from that infuriating experience: if you want to move up, you must make yourself known. Work and lurk in the shadows, and you'll probably stay there while others take credit for your results.

Executive coach Dee Soder, founder of the executive advisory and assessment firm The CEO Perspective Group, points out a practical reality: senior-level executives typically have hundreds of people working under them. And as one CEO recently told Soder, "How in the world am I going to know if someone is doing a good job unless they tell me?" While results can sometimes be so obvious that they speak for themselves and catapult a career, don't count on that to happen. Look around your organization and you may notice that the most capable people are not always the ones who get promoted. Too often we think that consciously drawing attention to our work is selfish, unprofessional, and greedy. But making yourself known is not about obnoxiously promoting yourself in a blatantly self-serving, egotistical manner, but about providing information in a substantive, professional way that establishes a professional presence in front of the right people.

Moving up is is not solely about what you do but also about *who knows* what you do (and ultimately who cares about your professional growth). Results alone do not always ensure that the folks who can best help you move up are aware of your name and capabilities. If your direct boss is the only person who can pick you out of a crowd, then when it comes time for your boss's boss to assign a significant project, the assignment is probably going to someone else—someone more people recognize.

What Do You Want to Be Known For?

Just as most great brands have calculated marketing and advertising programs behind them, professional reputations are formed by conscious effort. Marketers spend months if not years perfecting their product's message and identity. As employees, we must take control of the professional messages we send and be aware of our own brand. Branding yourself is not a new concept, but it should be taken seriously; when you think about your brand early in your career, you're more likely to be known for the reputation you want.

Protect Your Reputation by Dictating It

The best time to start formulating your professional reputation is before you begin a new job. This does not have to be a massive undertaking—it can be as simple as sitting down for an hour or so and crafting a short description of the professional reputation or image you want to have in the future, be it in six months or five years, as well as the professional messages you must communicate to make that reputation reality.

Complete the following sentences:

- In one year I want my resume to include:
- After two years on the job I want to be known as:
- In three years I want others to know me as someone who:
- In five years I want to have accomplished:
- When colleagues talk about me, I want them to say:
- While working at this company, I do *not* want to be known for:

Finish each phrase with half a dozen succinct, one-line bulleted statements that fill only one page. This forces you to prioritize and internalize your goals and desired image. Don't worry about repeating yourself, as redundancy only reinforces what is important to you.

No need to look at your answers every day, but keep the list accessible and reread it regularly. Eventually, your branding points embed themselves into your psyche. Every day, as you face major and minor decisions, they will automatically inform your choices. For example, if you do not want to be known as a busy bee, you will say no to busy work. If in three years you want to be known as a deal closer, you will ask to play key roles at sales presentations. If in one year you want to be known as a strategic thinker, you will communicate in the context of the big picture, even when you are working on simple daily tasks. The brand you want to create for yourself—a visionary, a team leader, a powerful communicator, an influential writer—will affect which projects you accept, what you talk about, how you talk, and where you choose to focus energy and spend time.

Your list of self-statements is sort of like a map to your professional life. It keeps you on target, cultivating the reputation you want to establish, and it prevents you from becoming known for traits you don't care about or skills that won't help you move up (such as a great note taker, a party planner, a gossip, an introvert, or "that woman in marketing who always wears plaid").

◆ **What it takes:** Articulate to yourself specific qualities for which you want to be known. Your personal brand map will help you focus on your intentions and prevent you from becoming known for other, less desirable traits.

Be Known for Traits That Are "Uniquely You"

Set realistic, attainable aspirations for yourself instead of trying to be known for something your skills cannot accommodate. For example, if you are not a particularly good public speaker, do not volunteer to talk in front of large groups; do so and you'll become known as a mediocre presenter. In contrast, if you are a solid writer, volunteer to create presentations and write strategic reports. Why highlight a weakness? Instead, identify a natural talent and pursue opportunities that require that talent. Not only will your performance shine, you will become known for your unique strengths.

A product manager named Amy McHaney works at a major airline buying expensive products for plane interiors, such as chair-back video screens. Amy believes her upbeat personality and outgoing nature is a unique asset in her organization's relatively conservative culture, and over the years she has made a conscious effort to highlight it. Whenever Amy's department wants to add features to a plane, she and her colleagues must seek executive approval, and Amy always volunteers to present to the executive committee. In addition to making sure she knows the products cold—knowledge that people with any personality type could easily master—Amy "puts on a show," as she likes to say, by using her confidence, enthusiasm, and expressive spirit to drive home messages to her audience. As a result, Amy has created a name for herself with key executives by combining her positive, high energy level with her knowledge and professionalism.

At one company, I developed a professional reputation as a problem solver and a "turn around" account manager, and as a result I was often thrown onto problem accounts. Once, when en route to

London (my first trip to England) for a prospective client meeting, I received a call from an executive who said, "Amy, we've got an emergency and we need you to help turn an account around. We think you are the only person who can do it." You'd better believe that, instead of continuing on to London, I immediately rerouted myself and took a bumpy prop plane down to a dreary manufacturing town in Tennessee. I put my tour of Buckingham Palace on hold for an opportunity to sharpen my professional brand. After all, Buckingham Palace wasn't going anywhere.

◆ **What it takes:** Play up unique strengths and play down weaknesses.

Be Known for Leadership Traits

Whether or not your goal is to serve in a management capacity, being known for leadership qualities can help you move up. Soder's proprietary research identified traits that are essential to leaders. Review the following list of traits, which are particularly important for women, and ask yourself:

1. Do you have *and* apply these traits?
2. Do people throughout your company know you for these qualities?

Optimism: You are enthusiastic and exude a zest for life. Others feed off your high level of energy, particularly when faced with problems.

A Willingness to Risk: You are willing to take on challenges, even when there is a high risk of failure. Soder says many women attain senior positions by successfully taking over a troubled division or an account that was considered a loser. Like it or not, women must prove themselves more than men, and one of the best and most high-profile ways to do so is by fixing high-profile problems.

A Self-Evaluating Nature: You seek feedback from others, both subordinates and superiors, and strive to improve yourself. Others feel comfortable approaching you with critiques and know you will take them constructively rather than personally. According to Dr. Soder, lack of feedback is one of the biggest problems holding women back. Make sure you know how you are performing in others' eyes.

Willingness to Work Hard: You are willing to put in the extra hours, make that extra phone call. A willingness to work hard does not negate working smart—longer does not always equal better—but you are known for going the extra mile as opposed to doing the bare minimum.

Play the Hand You're Dealt: You accept that while you cannot always determine what happens to you—even though your odds increase when you speak up and step up—you can determine how you will approach a given situation.

◆ **What it takes:** No matter what your goal, develop leadership qualities to assist in your quest for success.

What Not *to Be Known For*

Just as you plot positive traits you want to be known for, make a conscious effort to avoid negative characteristics that may overshadow your talents. Don't do the following:

- arrive late
- seek constant approval
- lack direction
- consistently leave work early
- take a long time to make decisions
- require micromanagement

- speak inappropriately and without thinking
- cry in public
- ramble
- come off as arrogant
- slack off and fail to complete assignments
- whine
- gossip
- show up to work unkempt
- chat the day away
- dress in a sexy manner
- flirt
- brownnose
- waste time doing busy work
- complain

I'm sure you can add your own to the list—just look around your office.

◆ **What it takes:** Remember that avoiding negative behaviors is as important as cultivating positive ones.

How to Make Yourself Known: Delivering the Message

Once you know which traits you want to be known for, there are several ways—in addition to doing excellent work—to help ensure you are known for the brand you want.

Get Face Time

To establish your professional presence, you must be physically present so key decision-makers know who you are and what you do. People tie results to a face, and the more they see you the easier it is for them to tie your face to what you do. To this end, look for opportunities to talk with superiors face-to-face. For example, had I attended even one status meeting with my company's senior executives when my client was having trouble, my team—and not just my boss—might have been recognized for its work. On *The Apprentice*, everyone feared going into the boardroom to face Donald Trump because only people in the boardroom risked being fired. But as Nick Warnock—who went into and survived the boardroom most often—pointed out, the boardroom is the only place to have a one-on-one interaction with the organization's primary decision-maker, Trump himself.

LouAnn, a former business development director, recalls that she got face time with her company's CEO by, in addition to her regular responsibilities, initiating high-profile company partnerships with large organizations, such as Microsoft. LouAnn's deals were so complex and high profile that they required her to constantly talk with senior management. "I had numerous meetings with the CEO not only to seek his approval, but to advise him so he could communicate the value of the strategic deals to the investment community." In short, she created the opportunity to make herself known. And her strategy worked. She was promoted to a senior director position in less than a year.

◆ **What it takes:** Look for opportunities to communicate in person with senior people. Even one meeting can make a difference.

Communicate Up

I had been at Commerce One for about a year, working diligently at customers' sites but only once visiting Commerce One's headquarters. That pattern changed after I serendipitously learned a tactic others in my office used. At a regional Commerce One meeting, I met a woman who I'd heard through the office grapevine was a superstar. In my mind, I pictured this woman having more than twenty years experience, always acting extremely serious, wearing conservative suits with hose, and having graying hair. When I finally met her in person I was shocked to see she was not only about my age, but had shoulder-length strawberry blond hair and was quite spunky and spirited. What's more, her level in the organization was relatively equal to mine. As I observed her, I found it fascinating that she chatted breezily with senior management and that they seemed truly pleased to see her and talk shop.

I thought to myself, "I'm doing something wrong." How was I going to make myself known and move up when no one except my immediate supervisor and my regional technical team knew anything about me? My performance was good, but except for my boss, no one knew or cared—and I certainly wasn't chatting it up with senior management. Worse, my boss at the time was somewhat introverted and definitely not a person I could count on to sing my praises to his superiors.

A few months later I jumped at an opportunity to work on a project with the "superstar" because I wanted to see her in action. Here is what I observed: she did not just manage accounts—she managed information, voluntarily talking about her clients with senior people. It was not unusual for her to be on the phone daily with vice presidents, asking their opinions (admit what you don't know *and* stroke egos), filling vice presidents in on potential risks (no surprises), and updating them on her accounts (speaking up about progress). She was not only chatting about the weather or last night's game; this superstar was *networking with substance*. By communicating critical messages about her account to senior management, she made sure everyone up to and including the president recognized her as a key champion for the customer—a reputation I am sure she was consciously cultivating. Yet she never made executives feel that she was wasting their time. She was succinct and confident in her delivery, and her messages always focused on relevant details and, more important, big-picture issues to demonstrate her critical thinking and vision.

Human resources manager Danielle Royston consults with employees who, she says, are not satisfied with their career growth because they lack what Royston refers to as organizational savvy. She says that employees often mistakenly assume they can put themselves on the "move-up" map by good work alone. "I ask frustrated people how they promote themselves, and it's sad because they just assume management has a crystal ball and is checking up on their progress."

It is easier to get in front of senior executives in smaller, or so-called flat, organizations where fewer rules of professional convention exist and where hierarchies don't separate employees from management as much. Companies in the technology sector tend to be flat, mainly because it's a young, fast-paced industry and decisions must be made quickly; its leaders also tend to be younger and closer in age to the workforce as well as less familiar (or concerned) with formal organizational structure, where workers only communicate with their immediate supervisors.

At larger companies, where you can't just pop your head into the CEO's office, you must make yourself known through more established procedures. Take advantage of these opportunities. At my first job, I was responsible for, among other tasks, preparing my department's biweekly status report, which circulated to the company's senior executives. I literally had to beg colleagues in my department to update me about their activities so I could roll the information into my report. People were too busy working to tell their bosses what they were accomplishing! They should have been *begging* me to include their name in the report so the "big guys" (yes, they were primarily men) would know about their productivity. The point to understand here is that it is easy to shirk what seems like busy work when, really, it is an important chance to make yourself known.

I love the secrets Royston shared with me on how she advises others to stealthily brag to the people who can help advance their careers:

1. Distribute e-mails that softly tout your accomplishments but are disguised as a status reports.
2. Verbally communicate positive progress by using language such as, "Let me update you on what we've accomplished. . . ."
3. Verbally communicate potential risks management should be aware of. Surface and address the issue, and you get credit for thinking "big picture."

Ultimately, you are responsible for managing your own career; communicating up is a key element to ensure growth. To illustrate this, private investor Kathy Elliott told me that no one comes to you with a career ladder, holds it up to the wall, and pulls you up it; you have to do that yourself. You've got to climb the ladder by making your accomplishments known—all the way to the top.

◆ **What it takes:** To move up, make sure you communicate to managers beyond your boss.

Overcome Intimidation

Regardless of whether your company has established procedures for communicating with senior management or an open-door policy, sometimes you have to be creative, bold, and spontaneous to make yourself known. My early attempts at making myself known were, well, nonexistent. I treated senior executives like royalty—avoiding eye contact and treating everything they said as gospel.

One summer, I was the sole intern in the marketing department at the headquarters office of Mary Kay cosmetics in Dallas. One day I walked into the restroom to see the most senior marketing executive washing her hands. Yes, the bathroom is a quasi-private place, but it was a perfectly good spot to introduce myself. I could have easily said, "Hi, I'm Amy the intern." She probably would have asked what I was working on, and I could have talked about some of the interesting projects I was involved with, like conducting competitive analysis for wrinkle-control products and researching and writing a makeover video for customers. But because I feared I was not worthy of her time, I avoided the opportunity and instead kept my eyes on the floor and practically ran into the nearest stall. I couldn't even muster a faint hello. Such silence was common for me back then, and it ensured that no one but my immediate boss knew how I spent my day. For all everyone else knew, I was the intern filing papers and fetching coffee.

A few years later, I had grown more courageous. Commerce One was a fast-growing start-up attracting senior executives from well-known companies. We grew from approximately 150 employees when I started to more than four thousand within a year and a half, and people who had been at Commerce One from the early days were no longer on a first-name basis with the company's new leadership team. Two weeks after a new president joined, I boarded an employee bus after a biannual customer meeting in New Orleans, and there, in one of the front rows, was the new president, with an empty seat next to him. Many employees were walking right past him, probably too intimidated to sit down next to the new chief, and either assumed they had nothing to say or that he had no interest in them. To me, the empty seat said, "opportunity to make yourself known." I stopped. "Is anyone sitting here?" I asked. He said "No, please have a seat." I introduced myself, and we began chatting about my role at Commerce One. He asked about my clients, so I told him about their accomplishments and challenges. Because he was new to the company I think he appreciated the level of detail. I had the president's ear for the half-hour drive to the customer awards dinner.

I know sitting next to the president on a bus isn't going to get me promoted. But it was a rare opportunity to have my voice—one of four thousand—heard by a senior person. By using this random opportunity to put my face with my name, I knew I would be more likely to be recognized for accomplishments when my clients' names came up down the road.

When I ran into the president a month later he didn't recognize me at first, but after I reintroduced myself he said, "Oh yes, on the bus in New Orleans. You look different. Your hair was straight then but it's curly now." I joked and said that I was having such challenges with my customers that it was making my hair curl. From then on it became a joke, and whenever I saw him at corporate functions he'd kid, "Oh, we must be making progress, your hair is straight again." Actually, it was more than a joke. After lighthearted banter, he usually congratulated me on my clients' specific milestones, which he had apparently heard about.

◆ **What it takes:** Use every unexpected opportunity to make yourself known among the senior ranks.

Create a Personal Sound Bite

A brief, memorable message encapsulating your character and skills can go a long way toward making your personal brand more widely known. For *The Apprentice*, I was constantly described as a ruthless businesswoman with a Southern sense of charm, thanks to my quote on NBC's website. I cannot tell you how many times that description was used in articles and how many people still come up to me and say, "Hello, ruthless businesswoman." It was a great description for television but hardly the image I wanted off the air. A memorable message can set you apart from others—just make sure it conveys the right message. If you don't want to be known forever as ruthless—or sweet, or nice, or accommodating—then get busy constructing the message you desire.

Mackenzie works in the mortgage lending business and has made a conscious effort to distinguish herself as a high-end consultant rather than a mass-market loan officer. She uses this sound bite whenever she speaks to real estate agents who can refer business her way: "I provide high-end buyers with sophisticated and tailored solutions that integrate to their short- and long-term financial and cash flow objectives." This targeted sound bite helps ensure Mackenzie gets referred to the high-end clients she seeks.

One thing I see over and over that I find perplexing: most of us easily use descriptive language and telling messages when we interview for a job, but we quickly abandon those messages once we land the job and walk into the office. Yet while we may have sold our image—and ourselves—to the few people who hired us, we have yet to sell ourselves to colleagues, clients, and other senior executives. We forget that many of our colleagues have yet to form an opinion about us and that our sound bite will continue to be useful in the office. In the context of dating, I often joke that once couples get serious, the "marketing stage" of the relationship often ends, meaning the flowers, cards, and sweet voice messages dwindle. Just as couples should continue to sell themselves to each other to keep romance alive, the same is true for work relationships—never stop selling yourself.

One way to succinctly communicate your professional message—
or what you want to be known for—is to develop an elevator pitch,
a 15-second description of your job or a current project, that you
can zip off while traveling from the first to tenth floor with the
CEO. This is where the language of your professional sound bite
is important. I would never introduce myself to the CEO on
the elevator and say, "Hi, I'm Amy Henry, a ruthless businesswoman with a Southern sense of charm." (I cringe just thinking
about how ridiculous this sounds.) I would, however, be prepared
to say, "Hi, I'm Amy Henry, the strategic accountant manager for
the global IBM account. You may already know, but because of
the customized software solutions we implemented, IBM has been
a great reference for us. Looks like we may have a long relationship
with Big Blue."

The tone and language in which you describe your job com-
municates a great deal about you as a professional. And when
you subtly add how your daily activities are affecting the overall
company (in my fictitious elevator scenario, creating a solid part-
nership with one of the world's largest companies), you show
awareness of company goals and vision, in addition to having a
handle on daily, tactical activities.

◆ **What it takes:** Plan, create, and then maintain a powerful sound
bite describing your professional self.

Tell Stories

If the sound bite approach isn't working for you, there is another way to talk about who you are and what you do: tell stories.
Anecdotes show us in action, are fun to hear, and can be more
memorable. Stories that communicate positive traits can be from
your personal or professional life. These days, many job interviews

ask you to recount stories of times when you, for example, solved a problem or showed initiative. Personal stories are particularly good when you are just entering the workforce and do not yet have much business experience.

Sharing a personal story worked well for me when I applied to graduate school. My applications were due before I found out the results of my GMAT scores, and initially I was concerned that my standardized test scores would not be high enough to warrant a substantial scholarship; my practice tests always placed me around the eightieth and ninetieth percentile, not high enough to earn a full ride. Regardless of my score, I did not believe that a standardized test could ever begin to translate the diligence and competitive spirit that I always applied to my work and that ensured I excelled. I did not know how to memorably and positively convey in the application that, while my scores might not be as high as other scholarship-worthy applicants, I had something people with higher scores might not have: drive and a commitment to excellence. My solution? I answered one of the application's questions with a personal story to convey the message. This, essentially, is what I wrote:

I remember the first time I ran a mile. In high school, I played volleyball but never ran. One time, our volleyball team was losing to another team and our coach threatened that if we did not beat "those losers" we would have to run a mile for every point by which we lost. When we lost by 11 points, I panicked. Not only had I never attempted to run a mile, I didn't think I'd even be able to get around the track one time without needing to stop and catch my breath. I had never been a long-distance runner; I only ran sprints. The coach made us a deal: if we ran the first mile in under nine minutes, we were off the hook.

Determined to meet her challenge, I huffed and puffed and crossed the finish line at eight minutes and 53 seconds. I felt like I had run a marathon, and after that I decided to turn that ever-so-dreaded activity into a new hobby.

I began running regularly and in college started taking group classes. My first semester "final exam" was running a five-kilometer race, which I still consider one of my greatest feats! Over the next few years I slowly boosted my endurance—running on my own in the mornings—until I had participated in my first of several half marathons and began training for marathons. Through perseverance, I had conquered my fear of long-distance running and turned it into a passion.

I hoped that the story of my evolving romance with running would convey that I was willing to work hard to overcome limitations—be it a mile, a marathon, or an accounting class. Ultimately, my test scores were much better than I expected; I was invited to interview and I was not only admitted but received a full scholarship. While in school, a few professors joked around and during classes called me the "huffin' and puffin' runner." One professor even referred to a class assignment as being "tougher than that first mile, eh?" My memorable message not only got me the "job," it helped me become known to my "bosses."

Stories that illustrate professional skills are everywhere—from sports to summer jobs to family experiences. How you deal with people and challenges in non-business settings can effectively communicate your value in business.

◆ **What it takes:** Use stories as a comfortable and memorable way to communicate and translate your professional image.

Let Dress Convey How You Want to Be Known, But Don't Be Known for How You Dress

Your dress is the visual expression of your brand. Are you conservative with a twist? Artistic? All business? Do not wear clothes that contradict or confuse the message you want to convey about yourself, especially when you are trying to establish credibility.

First Impressions

Especially when you first begin working at a company, err on the side of too formal and understated. Former computer industry executive Donna recounts how she kept her hot pink or bright red suits on hold until she achieved a reputation for her expertise at the traditional technology company. Bold clothing makes bold statements ("look at me" or "pay attention to me") and too much interest in your physical appearance can draw attention away from your mind. In the early years, you want your clothing to blend in more than stand out—Donna claims she wore taupe suits so bland they seemed void of color and ultimately forced others to focus on nothing other than her verbal messages.

◆ **What it takes:** Save the snazzy attire for *after* you've made yourself known.

The Clark Kent Maneuver

There will, of course, be days when you are not wearing your most professional attire to the office; days you look fine but not fabulous. These will also be the days, I guarantee, when you will be called into a last minute sales presentation or have a chance to go to lunch with your boss or the CEO. Too many times I've declined invitations to last minute meetings—all opportunities to make myself known among the senior rankings—because my attire wasn't professional enough. If you simply can't think without your comfy clothes on, have a spare suit and pair of shoes stashed in the office so you can morph from shabby to sharp in minutes.

Make an Effort to Know Others and Make Others Known

As you seek out senior management to assist your ascent, you should also help people below you and even equal to you on the corporate ladder. Do it for altruistic reasons—good work deserves to be recognized. Do it for practical reasons—networking is how people get ahead in business. And do it for personal reasons—making others known helps make you known.

Take a Genuine Interest

A genuine person takes an interest in her colleagues and doesn't just operate on automatic pilot or treat others mechanically. While there's an appropriate line between personal and professional, it's perfectly acceptable—as well as an effective management style—to connect with employees on a safe personal level. Coworkers will appreciate your interest, and you'll be known as a human being as well as a businesswoman.

Even slightly personalizing your professional relationship goes a long way toward improving communication and improving others' performance. After all, people tend to perform well for bosses they like as well as respect. If taking an interest doesn't come naturally and you are simply not the type who gives a hoot about coworkers' lives outside the office, understand that you do not have to be well versed in their life story or spend endless minutes chatting about their wedding, their new baby, or their new sports car. Just find some common ground you can share, or at least one topic you feel comfortable inquiring about—the college they attended, the team they root for, how the new baby is doing.

Once you get information, don't forget it. First, there is nothing more embarrassing and insincere than asking someone how their kids are when they have none, or how a man's wife is if he is gay. I'm sure you've had dates when the guy can't remember where you grew up even though you've told him a dozen times.

Specifics make people feel appreciated and remembered: "How's your son, little Ryan?" I asked an attorney with whom I'm currently negotiating a deal with. "How's the margarita-selling business?" I inquired of a business executive I ran into recently. "What's the latest gadget purchase?" I asked a developer at my company who is known for splurging on technical devices. "How's the yoga coming along?" I queried an acquaintance I ran into in the store. "Still liking the lime green Volkswagen?" I joked with an old colleague I spoke with recently.

Granted, asking about others is not rocket science, but I cannot tell you how many managers I've seen that do not care to know anything about the people with whom they work every day. Business may not be personal, but having a genuine interest and communicating that interest helps you develop and maintain relationships and makes you known in the most positive of ways.

◆ **What it takes:** Let others know they are known by you.

Broadcast Others' Accomplishments

Praise others and they will praise you. Not only do people appreciate positive feedback (just as you do) but it makes you known as an effective leader and encourages the people you lead to credit you, too. And even if you don't manage people, you should still be cognizant of making an effort to acknowledge peers' good work. In fact, unsolicited compliments are often the most appreciated. For example, marketing manager Lauren is a constant recommender. She touts people's expertise and connects them with people who need it:

From professional recommendations ("my friend is a brilliant mortgage agent") to personal ("I know someone who just returned from the same Greek island you are visiting"), I always follow up with an e-mail to both parties to connect them. It builds a relationship with the recommended person, and also I find that I get professionally recommended more often in exchange.

As a project manager, I routinely sent out company-wide or targeted e-mails recognizing my team's successes. Of course, I copied my entire team on the e-mail, and I named names—"Adam was critical to the on-site implementation, Jamie was instrumental in configuring the application, Kim provided superior customer service, Joanie delivered first-class training, Ches and his team developed flawless customizations, and my executive sponsor, Andy, provided superior guidance and escalation support." I usually kept my personal contribution out of the e-mail and let my team's accomplishments speak for me. Not only did my teams appreciate the e-mails, but I always heard back from senior executives with congratulations. I got credit as a leader and my team got credit for their contributions. One word of advice: always, always credit your boss, so that your boss doesn't feel you are attempting to surpass authority or take his or her job (even if you are).

◆ **What it takes:** Do not underestimate the value of praising others. It's good for them and good for you.

You've Made a Name for Yourself—Embrace It!

Eventually, you will be known for your talents, your intellect, and your creative ideas, and people will credit you accordingly, as well as compliment you on projects well done or problems well solved. Hear this now: resist the urge to downplay accolades!

Women do this *all the time.* Someone tells us, "You look fabulous," and we say, "Oh please, I didn't even do my hair." They say, "Congratulations on landing the account," and we reply, "Oh, it was nothing, I was just lucky." This female instinct to fend off compliments is counterproductive, comes off as insecurity, and erases all the effort you've put into making yourself known. Train yourself, force yourself, to simply say, "Thank you." You did the work, you earned the reputation as well as the compliment—accept it.

I have a hard time taking compliments gracefully, so I play with sarcasm: "Oh, go on, go on . . ." or "Oh, darling, keep the compliments coming." It's much better than "Oh, stop." You just might get what you ask for, and you don't really want the compliments to stop coming, do you? I know I don't.

Conclusion

During the process of writing this book, I went to church one Sunday and heard the preacher share with the congregation a parable that ended with the following Bible verse: "Seed fell on good soil. It came up and yielded a crop, a hundred times more than was sown" (Luke 8:8). It reminded me of a story I wrote more than twenty years ago.

What It Takes is my first book, but it is not the first time I attempted to have my writing published. At age 11, I wrote a story about a flower for my sixth grade class, and my grandmother, on encouragement from my teacher, sent the piece to publishing houses only to receive a handful of very polite rejection letters. My grandmother recently mailed me a copy of my story she had saved all these years, and its innocent theme struck me as apropos to *What It Takes*. Here's what I wrote in 1984:

> *One day in March I was walking down Blueberry Street when I noticed a beautiful flower. Every day I started coming by to sing to it. One day when I came by to sing to it, it said, "I love you." I said, "What?" "I love you," it said. "Every day you come by and sing to me and that makes me very happy and beautiful."*

I came by every day for about four months—then one day the flower disappeared. I thought to myself, "Someone must have picked it." When I was walking home I noticed it lying in the gutter by a bag of dead grass and flowers. I picked it up, brought it home, and then planted it.

The flower grew and grew until one very cold day in September it died. I buried it on the side of our backyard. Months passed, and it was finally March. I was outside kicking my soccer ball when I noticed a sprout from where I had buried my flower. I was so happy that my friend, the flower, had come back to life!

A simple story with a simple message: like flowers, careers must be nurtured. A successful career does not just sprout overnight. Your career is a process that unfolds over the course of a lifetime, and like water to a flower, the techniques in *What It Takes* are food for your career's growth. They should become part of your routine as a businesswoman, woven into every job and every day on the job. Speaking up, stepping up, and making yourself known help you blossom. Building relationships grows your network. Valuing your worth helps you prosper. Choosing objectivity over emotion cultivates professionalism, and using your own inherently feminine traits keeps you true to your roots.

And staying true to your roots—the talents and personality that make you unique—is key. I do not want you to change who you are. So even if some of the ideas in *What It Takes* seem like bold departures from how you typically conduct yourself at work, don't let those feelings of discomfort stop you from being proactive. These techniques do not require you to change the person you are—just the opposite. Everything in *What It Takes* is about sowing and harvesting your existing skills and ensuring that you are rewarded for your talents, time, and energy. As you continue to grow, you will be empowered to become a better and stronger version of yourself.

Your career will have many seasons over the course of your lifetime, and throughout the seasons you must not only adapt to changing conditions—coworkers' personalities, stereotypes, office cultures, economic shifts—but take control of your own professional growth. That is what it takes for all of us to move up in our careers. I wish you every success and hope you flourish.

For more information on Amy Henry,
to schedule her to speak at your next event, or to find a
reading group guide,
please visit www.ameliahenry.com.

	DATE DUE		